I'll Hold You In Heaven
Remembrance Book

When you ask a woman how many children she has, women in developing countries count them all—then they tell you how many are still alive. In our "developed" country, we still struggle to face the grief of a lost child. Debbie Heydrick's book acknowledges the grief of a mother who has a child waiting in heaven, and speaks to her from shared experiences. I will buy several copies to have on hand so that I am ready to help those who often grieve silently.

DALE HANSON BOURKE
SENIOR VICE PRESIDENT, WORLD RELIEF
AUTHOR, *EVERYDAY MIRACLES* AND *TURN TOWARD THE WIND*

The Baylor Foundation is very supportive of the concept of Angels in Heaven Ministries and recommend it without reservation.

CHARLES M. COOPER
PRESIDENT, BAYLOR HEALTH CARE SYSTEM FOUNDATION

As a pediatrician who has learned the sorrow of infant death, I heartily endorse *I'll Hold You in Heaven Remembrance Book*. The keepsake element is a wonderful way of helping turn grief, following the loss of a child, into the joy of knowing that God cares.

WILLIAM R. FACKLER, M.D.
FORMER CHIEF OF STAFF AND BOARD MEMBER, BAYLOR RICHARDSON MEDICAL CENTER

One of the most devastating losses that a family can face is the loss of a child, whether born or unborn. Out of this pain comes a desire by the family to acknowledge the life that was lost. Words alone are seldom adequate to communicate either the depth of the loss or the significance of that life to those who were touched by it. Family and friends surrounding the grieving parents look for ways to reach out and minister. I am excited about the development of *I'll Hold You in Heaven Remembrance Book*. In my 40+ years of ministry, I have seen few ministerial tools designed to help those suffering from this type of loss. I am sure this keepsake will touch your heart as it has mine.

Dr. Gene A. Getz
Senior Pastor, Fellowship Bible Church North
Director, Center for Church Renewal

Reading *I'll Hold You in Heaven Remembrance Book* is like the tender touch and shared sorrow of a best friend who understands. Through the pages of this helpful book, Debbie Heydrick walks with those who have lost a child and offers the gentle direction and encouragement only one who has been to that painful place can give.

Nancy Guthrie
Author, *Holding On to Hope*

How many do you suppose will be helped in the future through the words of comfort and pictures of love in *I'll Hold You in Heaven Remembrance Book*? I praise God for you, your gift of encouragement to me and for all the many people's lives you will touch through this awesome ministry.

The Heidi Group

An important and often hard-learned spiritual truth is that our tragedies and
crises can be used by God to help others through the same situations. Some never comprehend
the power to help that is resident within them. Others, however, embrace the opportunity.
Debbie Heydrick is such a person.

After suffering one miscarriage, Debbie, and her husband, Douglas, founded a ministry to
help parents through the loss of an infant due to miscarriage and stillbirth. Many have been helped through
this ministry, and with the release of Debbie's first book, *I'll Hold You in Heaven Remembrance Book*,
many more will find comfort and support through this most difficult time.

In this book, Debbie compassionately validates the importance of the life lost
(no matter how short-lived). I strongly recommend this book to those who have suffered
this type of loss and to those who love them.

JOSH D. MCDOWELL
AUTHOR, SPEAKER

I'll Hold You In Heaven
Remembrance Book

DEBBIE HEYDRICK

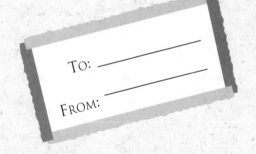

TO: _____

FROM: _____

Regal

From Gospel Light
Ventura, California, U.S.A.

PUBLISHED BY REGAL BOOKS
FROM GOSPEL LIGHT
VENTURA, CALIFORNIA, U.S.A.
PRINTED IN THE U.S.A.

Regal Books is a ministry of Gospel Light, an evangelical Christian publisher dedicated to serving the local church. We believe God's vision for Gospel Light is to provide church leaders with biblical, user-friendly materials that will help them evangelize, disciple and minister to children, youth and families.

It is our prayer that this Regal book will help you discover biblical truth for your own life and help you meet the needs of others. May God richly bless you.

For a free catalog of resources from Regal Books/Gospel Light, please call your Christian supplier or contact us at 1-800-4-GOSPEL *or* www.regalbooks.com.

Cover and interior design by Robert Williams
Edited by Deena Davis

Library of Congress Cataloging-in-Publication Data
Heydrick, Debbie.
    I'll hold you in heaven remembrance book / Debbie Heydrick.
        p. cm.
    ISBN 0-8307-3260-8
    1. Children—Death—Religious aspects—Christianity—Meditations. 2.
Parents—Prayer-books and devotions—English. 3. Consolation.   I.
Title.
    BV4907.H44 2003
    248.8'66—dc21   2003004696

1   2   3   4   5   6   7   8   9   10   11   12   13   14   15   /   09   08   07   06   05   04   03

Rights for publishing this book in other languages are contracted by Gospel Light Worldwide, the international nonprofit ministry of Gospel Light. Gospel Light Worldwide also provides publishing and technical assistance to international publishers dedicated to producing Sunday School and Vacation Bible School curricula and books in the languages of the world. For additional information, visit www.gospellightworldwide.org; write to Gospel Light Worldwide, P.O. Box 3875, Ventura, CA 93006; or send an e-mail to info@gospellightworldwide.org.

DEDICATION

To our precious baby, Julia, lost through miscarriage on
August 4, 1994, and most recently, to our multiple losses through
miscarriage on November 25, 2002. Our lives are forever changed
because you were here. Your brief lives were gifts from above
and continue to impact lives for Christ, even now.

To my loving husband and my inspiration, Doug, who laughs with me,
cries with me, grieves with me and loves me unconditionally.
I love you, my forever friend.

To my five precious children—Jessica, Jonathan, Jacob, Joshua
and Julie—my gifts from God, who have joyfully made countless sacrifices
of mommy time, allowing me the quiet moments I needed to pray,
to think and to write. Thank you, children.

To Pastor Jack Hayford, my friend, for your life-giving book I'll Hold You in
Heaven, which brought so much comfort to us during our time of loss.

To my precious friends and family; without your prayers and
support this book could not have happened. Thank you for believing in me
and holding me up through all the difficult days.

DEAR READER

My prayer is that this book will be a companion in your
journey of loss, pain, healing and hope. Please know that if
you will let Him, God binds up the brokenhearted, comforts
all who mourn, provides for all who grieve. He wants to
do this for you. Let Him give you a crown of beauty instead
of ashes, the oil of gladness instead of mourning,
a garment of praise instead of despair.

CONTENTS

Part 1: A Crown of Beauty Instead of Ashes

Part 2: The Oil of Gladness Instead of Mourning

Part 3: A Garment of Praise Instead of Despair

Part 4: Stories of Loss, Healing and Hope

FOREWORD

A quiet awakening is taking place. There is a softer and more penetrating voice being lifted amidst the thunder of strife and voices of discord making a battleground of the issues of a woman's rights and an unborn child's right to life.

This voice is one of comfort offering a healing warmth to those who, beyond and outside the arguments, have found that the loss of their unborn or infant child has left a relentless ache surrounding a painful void.

The voice whispers from heaven through the words and writings of people more interested in offering hope than in winning an argument. To them, it isn't a matter of analyzing how the child's life concluded—stillbirth, miscarriage, abortion, SIDS. Their concern is with the present. They know that sooner or later the hurt and the questions arrive, and they simply hope to speak to those whose pain too often encounters only the trumpetings of the self-righteous, the unintended but no less painful barbs of the insensitive or, even worse, the empty silence of the disinterested.

Debbie Heydrick is one of those soft voices. Hers is a gentle voice filled with strength gained through the wisdom of her own trying and painful experiences. It is a voice of sanity filled with truth mined from God's own heart of love for people and His tender mercies available to every aching heart.

Debbie's voice is worth listening to for many reasons, not the least of which is her own acquaintance with the pain and question marks that punctuate the passage of one's child before that life has had a chance to happen.

Within the hour I met Debbie and heard her and her husband's story, I encouraged her to write this book. I was certain that its counsel would provide dimensions of hope and healing needed more today than ever before. Now the book is in your hands, and as a pastor who has counseled thousands of people at various points of pain and perplexity, I guarantee you this book packages a resource of rich value.

The *genius* of the book is its accessibility—it not only speaks comfort but it also draws you into the process of fully realizing that comfort. That is because of the *genuineness* of the writer who has been there before, has found truly workable answers and has prepared this book as a tool to help you work through pain and find answers.

So go ahead. Read and receive comfort—take action, and watch hope begin to rise as your healing begins. If you will do that—if you will go ahead—I can assure you in advance of one thing more: You are about to become as thankful for this book's appearance as I am.

Jack W. Hayford

Founding Pastor, The Church On The Way
Chancellor, The King's College and Seminary
Van Nuys, California

PREFACE

As difficult as the past few months have been for me, I feel that it would be helpful for you to know where I have walked. I know the pain of loss. Eight years ago my husband and I lost, through miscarriage, a very wanted and loved baby whom we named Julia. Out of our pain and loss and the healing we received in Christ, a ministry was birthed. Angels in Heaven Ministries is a resource for people who have suffered the loss of a baby through miscarriage, stillbirth, ectopic pregnancy or early infant death. We chose to name our ministry after the endearing term "angel." Although we know that little ones do not become angels when they die, it does feel as if we have entertained angels unaware.

For many years I have shared with hurting families the hope of Jesus Christ though the testimony and loss of our Julia. I plan to share more about our precious baby, so briefly with us, but first I have something else to tell you.

In late October 2002, during the final days of writing this book, I lost my father suddenly to a heart attack. Losing my daddy so unexpectedly was very difficult. I was reminded in a fresh and personal way of the pain of losing a treasured life. Then just a little more than a week later, I found that we were expecting. What joy filled our hearts! Doug and I were surprised yet very excited about this news. The joy of new life seemed so hopeful and healing to me yet bittersweet as I dealt with the painful loss of my daddy. As the days went by, our joy and anticipation grew.

We tried to contain our excitement for a few extra days as I waited for just the right time to share the news with our children (Jessica, 13; Jonathan, 12; Jacob, 9; Joshua, 7; and Julie, 4). I finally made the announcement to our oldest two children after much questioning and suspicion from them that something was up. They told us they had both been asking God for another baby for many, many months. How precious were their words! There are few things that bring more joy to Doug and me than to see our children loving, caring and praying for one another. My younger three children all shared in the excitement when we told them the news. My main thought was, *This is just what we needed! A new sweet baby to love.* Although Doug and I had not made a decision to grow our family at that time, we gladly welcomed the addition.

Day by day we became more excited about the gift of life God was blessing our family with. In growing anticipation, I began to gather maternity clothes and baby items and to make plans to accommodate a new little one in our family. I thought about how far along I would be on various special days coming up. I thought about the due date that would come soon after the release date of this book. I could hardly believe that my dream of sharing the message of God's comfort, healing and peace that He had placed within me was not only coming true but that I was also being blessed with another precious child.

A few weeks later, my oldest daughter and I went to the doctor to have my pregnancy confirmed and to have a sonogram. I was excited to see what was going on within me. I was growing so much more quickly than ever before and experiencing ligament pain already. We found that I was six-and-a-half weeks along, and to our great surprise, there were two pregnancy sacks and the shadow of another unconfirmed sack. We were so excited that so early in the pregnancy the doctor was able to see a baby and a heartbeat in one of the sacks. The doctor felt it was still very early and that in a week or so we should be able to see more clearly the baby in the second sack and find the baby's beating heart as well. My daughter and I left the doctor's office with great hope and joy.

It is amazing to me that a bond can happen so quickly between mother and baby, yet more amazing still is that children can open their hearts to love a new sibling and experience an attachment to that life as well. Jessica went home and began to write the most precious letters to our babies. Let me take you for a moment into the heart of my daughter Jessica. She, along with her brothers and sister, has grown up in a home that values life in the womb. We talk about the fragility of life as it grows within a mommy. We stop to pray when we see mothers carrying life and ask God for His protection over these precious lives. Here are some excerpts from letters Jessica wrote to our little one in hopes that this baby would soon join our family.

Friday, November 8, 2002

Dear Baby, I love you! I hope that you have a long life here on Earth with your family. I am your big sister. I have been waiting for you for a long time. You are a blessing from God. You are an answer to my prayers! I pray that our mommy has no complications with the pregnancy or the birth. I also pray that you are a very healthy baby when you are born. I will love you no matter what gender you are. Your birth date is supposedly going to be July 6, 2003. Oh, by the way, you may not be alone. Mommy thinks that you may be a twin. The joy is indescribable! I am so excited that I just want to scream and cry at the top of my lungs. I mean it! If you don't know, your mom's in the middle of writing a book. She is amazing! Lord, I know You are the only One who can give my mom a very healthy pregnancy and birth, so I pray to You. Lord Jesus, please give my mom the easiest pregnancy ever. Thank You! Amen.

Wednesday, November 12, 2002

Hi, Baby. I am so excited about having you as a new addition to our family. You are so loved and you're not even here yet. I am looking forward to teaching you a lot of stuff. I am going to be the best big sister. I can't wait to tell all my friends about you. They will be so surprised!

Thursday, November 13, 2002

I just wrote thoughts about you yesterday, but I have more thoughts about you today. I am still praying for you. I am going to stay up with you at night to feed you and change your diapers.

Your Big Sissy

After a time we went back to the clinic for another sonogram, but this time we found there was no longer any detectable heartbeat. The sacks had begun to shrink and be absorbed into my body, and only one lifeless form of a baby could be found. The other baby had stopped growing too early for us to physically see its tiny unformed body. The third sack had vanished without a trace. I quietly left the office after thanking the caring, compassionate nurse-technician for her time and her services.

As I sat in my car in the warm sunshine, knowing that I needed to get home and work on my book, I thought, *Could this really be happening? Where had my babies gone? They were here one moment and then gone the next. Was it all a dream? What now? So much loss and pain and uncertainty in my life.* At that moment, in the numbness of shock, just a few days before Thanksgiving, I had some big choices to make. Could I finish my book? Did I have anything left within me to give? Did the Lord, who began a good work in me, have plans to enable me to finish? Would the message and hope that God had placed deep within my heart stand firm through yet another raging storm? Could I go back through the manuscript in my brokenness and with all boldness still say that I believe its message of God's comfort, peace, healing and hope?

How would I make it through the next five days until my scheduled appointment with my doctor when I felt such uncertainty about the lives within me? What would I tell Doug and my children? Could the nurse-technician be wrong? I was anxious to have my doctor either confirm these findings or, as my optimistic self kept dreaming, tell me the babies were fine and it was all a big mistake. I chose to hold on to hope that anything was possible until it was confirmed that all hope was gone. The following were Jessica's journal entries during the next few days, and a note to the baby from me:

Friday, November 22, 2002

Hi. This is your big sister Jessica. I am so excited about you. You are why I am living each day with such joy right now. I really mean that! Please do not go to live in heaven with God yet. I really want you to stay here with me until we are really old. There are so many other people who want you to be here too.

Sissy

Friday, November 22, 2002

Hi, Baby. I am praying that you are able to come live here with me next summer. I am also praying that you are a very healthy baby. You are the most exciting thing in my life right now and I do not want this to become sad. Your mom will be going in for a sonogram again on Tuesday, next week. Yesterday she went and they could not find your heartbeat. I am really sad about that, but there is still hope that you are alive in there! Please hang in there for me and for the rest of our family.

Sissy

A note from Mommy

Saturday, November 23, 2002

Dear Baby,

We love you. We love you and we wish you a wonderful life—if not here, then in heaven. We are so glad we saw your heart beating, your sissy and I. I pray that if you are being ushered into heaven, then you will know our love for you and for your sister Julia, who is already waiting there for you. You may have a twin there too. Let sweet Jesus hold you till we are all there to hold you. We are glad you will have heaven and we are confident you will be there, but we will miss you greatly while we are apart. I still hope you can hang on to life. I want that more than anything right now. I will just wait to see what God has for us.

Your presence here has touched our whole family. Hundreds and thousands of lives will be touched by your life as well through the fresh perspective I have on the pain of loss as I finish my book. I was also reminded with a passion of the hope we have of seeing you and Julia in heaven someday—complete, whole and perfect.

Feel our love for you and our prayers for your precious life. Know that we treasure you.

Your mommy (and Big Sissy)

On a Monday night, November 25, 2002, a week before my manuscript deadline, I miscarried the first baby. The following Sunday night, I miscarried the second sack. I know I don't have to explain to you the pain of loss. Chances are great that if you're reading this book, you too know the pain of losing a life you were looking so forward to having in your family. Up until now, the story I had to share with you was that of Julia. The loss of Julia changed my life forever, setting me on a lifelong journey of healing and reaching out to comfort others with the comfort I had received in Christ (see 2 Cor. 1:3-4). Now I find myself eight years after Julia's loss—who was the catalyst for writing this book—facing the same tough questions I had faced when I lost her. She is no longer our only little one in heaven.

I write with even bolder confidence the message God has given me to share with you. I have lived it yet again, and I tell you that God is faithful! He has a plan, He is in control, and He cares. I am still so sad, and my family still grieves; but I tell you that God gives beauty for ashes, gladness for mourning and hope for despair—again and again and again. Once again I have a choice to become bitter or to grow through the process. I choose hope and joy. I choose to grow through the experience.

I pray that the pages of this remembrance book will be a blessing to you. I pray that they may open your eyes and heart to the healing and hope that waits for you. I pray that you will find boldness in choosing to remember your little one's life—a life worth remembering.

In Memory of

Our
Precious Baby

Psalm 139

Little Footprints

How very softly
you tiptoed into my world.
Almost silently,
only a moment you stayed.
But what an imprint
your footsteps have left
upon my heart.

Dorothy Ferguson

We'll hold you
in Heaven,

Your Family

Psalm 139:14

"I praise you because I am
fearfully and wonderfully made;
your works are wonderful,
I know that full well."

PART 1

A Crown of Beauty Instead of Ashes

Why

WORDS AND MUSIC BY DAVE CLARK, MARK HARRIS AND DON KOCH

They say that into every life some rain must fall
For the pain is no respecter of the mighty or the small
But sometimes it just seems so unfair
To see the one who's had more than his share
Oh it makes you wonder why

And Lord I wouldn't second guess your mighty plan
I know you have a purpose that's beyond the scope of man
If you look inside my heart you will find
That I have always been the trusting kind
Oh but still I wonder

Chorus:
Why—do the rainy days have to come
When the storm clouds hide the sun
I wanna know why
Why—when the reasons aren't clear to me
When it all is a mystery
I want to know why
And though down here I may not understand
I won't let go of the unseen hand
For it holds the reasons why

The Lord has never been afraid of honest prayers
And he won't allow the burden to be more than you can bear
When he knows that you're trust is in him
He doesn't mind the questions now and then
Even if you wonder

Chorus

CHAPTER ONE

FACING THE LOSS AND GRIEF

Though I walk in the midst of trouble, you preserve my life.

PSALM 138:7

The loss of a child, born or unborn, is perhaps the most difficult loss anyone could ever endure. This untimely and unnatural event can be so emotionally painful that it rocks the very core of your being. You may express your loss profoundly, grieving deeply and openly. You may be more reserved in your expression of grief, processing your feelings quietly and privately yet mourning every bit as much as those who are more openly expressive. You may find yourself somewhere in between. Everyone grieves differently and for varying lengths of time. Grief is personal, and it is unique to each person.

Wherever you are in your journey of loss, and no matter what emotions you might be experiencing at this time, I encourage you to embrace your grief. Mourning the loss of a life is natural, normal and healthy.

Know that the validity of your grief is not dependent on whether

- your loss was a result of miscarriage, ectopic pregnancy, stillbirth or early infant death;
- your baby's unformed body was deemed "viable" according to the medical world;
- you or your doctor physically saw your child's heart beating on a sonogram;
- your baby lived 4 weeks or 40 in the womb;
- your little one lived for a few days, weeks or months outside the womb;
- you held your baby or never had the chance;
- you experienced a sense of closure or had no real closure at all.

The fact is that you conceived life, and that life grew within you. The life of your baby deserves to be validated, and the loss of your hopes and dreams needs to be acknowledged. *Your baby's life was significant to you and is very significant to God.*

Maybe your loss occurred many years ago and you never felt free to grieve, or maybe your loss is quite recent. Maybe you are deeply saddened right now and feel the void of your little one's passing. Perhaps you feel numbness more than anything else, or you're not sure what you should feel. Though you may be afraid to admit it, perhaps you feel embarrassed for the depth of your emotion and sorrow over a life that was only with you, in the physical sense, for a very short time.

If you have never felt truly free to grieve, I want to give you permission to do that now. Your loss and your grief need your acknowledgment, your response and your acceptance. You must allow yourself full expression to feel the way that you feel. You have suffered a very significant loss—the loss of your very own child.

Not only have you lost your child, but you have also lost the hopes and dreams of what could have been. From the first few moments when we learn of the existence of life within us, our minds begin to think about how this new being will become an integral part of our lives. In just one moment you became Mommy and Daddy to a new life. You may have calculated how far along in the pregnancy you would be on special days such as Christmas or your birthday. You may have thought about the time of year you would deliver and even have begun making plans or changing plans to accommodate the impending arrival of your child. Then, in one moment, just as quickly as those exciting and hopeful thoughts had come, they were crushed with the reality of loss.

God is the author, creator and finisher of life. You need to know that the loss of your little one's life was not your fault. Trust in the fact that you did everything in your power to love and parent your baby. In extremely rare cases, where there might be room for doubt about the level of care that your baby received, *God is still sovereign!* Don't blame yourself or others unjustly. God has power over all human error and can exercise that power when it lines up with His plan.

The fact is that loss happens—and the number of occurrences are staggering. We can't even begin to understand all the whys; nor can we control the process of our losses. We can do everything in our human power and limited knowledge to sustain the life of our little ones, but life and death are ultimately up to God. For some reason, He has allowed your loss. You don't have to understand it; you need to trust that He has the best in mind for both you and your child. His ways are higher than our ways and He will fulfill His purposes through these precious lives He has created.

As difficult as it may be, facing your loss is the only way you can really begin to heal and see how something good can come out of something so incredibly difficult. I want to acknowledge your parenthood, the life and death of your baby and the reality and validity of your grief. Don't be embarrassed by the deep emotions you may experience over the passing of your child. Your grief is understandable, and the life of your baby is significant and worth remembering.

I want to acknowledge your parenthood, the life and death of your baby and the reality and validity of your grief.

I am so very sorry for your loss. I don't want you to think that you are all alone in your grief. Please know that God is more than able to handle your questions, disappointments and even the anger that might arise as a result of your loss. Run to Him now. He wants to reveal more of Himself to you and His love for you as you hold on to Him. You do not need to have all the answers; just trust in Him. In time, as you heal, you will begin to see the many ways you have been forever touched by your child's brief time with you. Allow your baby to leave his or her footprints on your heart.

PRAYER

Dear God, help us as we come

face-to-face with our loss. Let us

grieve unashamed, trusting that

our little one is now with You.

Help us accept our loss and grow

closer as a family. Let us day by

day begin to see Your plan. Help

us trust when we can't see

through the tears. Let us know

You are here. Amen.

J O U R N A L

Have you truly faced the pain of your loss? Have you allowed your heart to grieve? Try to put in writing, if only in a few words, how your heart honestly feels about your loss (e.g., sad, lonely, confused, angry, empty).

Taking steps toward recognizing how you are feeling inside and facing your pain is the beginning of healing. Take a moment and share where you are today in your grief.

_____

_____

_____

_____

_____

_____

_____

_____

_____

_____

_____

ANGEL UNAWARE

WORDS AND MUSIC BY SHARI BUIE AND TAMARA MILLER

Oh, the longing we both had
To be a mommy and a dad
We put our hopes and dreams in you
He hoped for pink, I dreamed of blue
But for you God had a different plan
One we may never understand

Chorus:
We were visited by an angel
Though we didn't know it then
You were the answer to our prayer
Our Angel Unaware

We hardly got to say hello
Before we had to let you go
God breathed your name and called you home
So briefly here, so quickly gone
But in the stillness of the night
My empty arms still hold you tight

In my mind I see you running,
Chasing bees and butterflies.
Soft hair gently blowing,
Healthy cheeks, laughing eyes.
In the quietness of the morning
When the mist hangs in the air,
I hold you close within my heart—
My Angel Unaware

How can I miss someone so much
I barely had the chance to touch
Yet as you grew inside of me
I learned how strong a love could be
I knew you for a lifetime
I'll love you all of mine

Chorus

CHAPTER TWO

FOCUSING ON THE FACTS

For you created my inmost being; you knit me together in my mother's womb.

PSALM 139:13

According to God's creative design, every unborn child has distinct spiritual significance. God knew all the days of your baby's life before any of those days (or moments) came to be. Before your baby was even conceived, God had a plan. Your baby was not a mere product of conception, a lump of tissue, or a life just not meant to be. Those words are painful to hear and deval-

ue the sanctity of life, and they are untrue. God *never* makes knitting mistakes when He knits life in the womb. From conception, your baby's life was truly human and therefore is an eternal soul—a life ordained by God Himself.

You are not alone in your loss. As shocking as it sounds, statistics show that 25 percent of all human conceptions do not complete the twentieth week of pregnancy. One in four pregnancies end in miscarriage. Seventy-five percent of fatal deaths of infants occur in the first twenty weeks.[1] These numbers are staggering. Why then are we made to feel that losses through miscarriage, ectopic pregnancy, stillbirth and early infant death are relatively uncommon happenings that only a few people experience? As statistics show, losses

> *God* never *makes knitting mistakes when He knits life in the womb.*

of this kind are far from rare. These numbers translate into empty arms, broken hearts and many childless parents.

A great number of people experience multiple losses. Whether it is your first loss or one of many, your loss is significant. Even if you already have children, the pain of losing a baby is crushing. Although I had three children when I miscarried, our family was deeply grieved by our loss. Each child is a special creation, and one child cannot replace another.

Before our own experience, my husband and I were not aware of the frequency of pregnancy loss. After we miscarried, our eyes were opened to the losses of others.

Although the world will try to downplay or even negate the significance of life in the womb, there is evidence that your little one was a very real presence. Just as there is evidence of wind and air—although we cannot see wind and air—there is evidence of your baby's existence. Life cannot pass through us without leaving its imprint of life in the womb.

What evidence do you have that validates the life of your child? There are many, including a pregnancy test, cravings, morning sickness, extreme tiredness, heartbeat sounds, sonogram pictures, body-shape changes, hormonal stress, baby hiccups and kicks, baby showers, gifts, pictures and videos.

As you seek validation for your little one's existence, I want to take you to God's Word. The Bible acknowledges and validates the significance of your child's brief life. It seems that thousands of years ago, God had already anticipated the problem of a world that would not acknowledge that life begins in the womb at the moment of conception. The Bible specifically describes and recognizes life during the first three months of pregnancy.

In Psalm 139:13-16, we see that God is the One who created life in the womb. He knows intimately each life conceived, even as He knows you now. These verses strongly validate all stages of life, from the very moment of conception as the substance of life to the fully formed life ready for delivery into the world:

> For you created my inmost being; you knit me together in my mother's womb. I praise you because I am fearfully and wonderfully made; your works are wonderful, I know that full well. My frame was not hidden from you when I was made in the secret place. When I was woven together in the depths of the earth, your eyes saw my unformed body. All the days ordained for me were written in your book before one of them came to be.

The same truths apply to you and your baby:

- God formed your delicate inner parts.
- You were woven together by God in your mother's womb.
- You were wonderfully and complexly made.
- You were not hidden from God when your frame was made in utter seclusion.
- God's eyes saw your very substance when you were yet unformed.
- Each day of your life was planned and recorded before your first moment of existence came to pass.

Life is God's creation, created to bring glory to Him. Although we can set up the circumstance for God to create a life, we do *not* make life happen; He does. Even before our babies are conceived, all of their days have been numbered. That means that each moment of our babies' existence here on Earth, whether in or out of the womb, whether for a few hours, days, weeks or months, was planned and allowed by God. He created that life just as He had planned. There is no room for happenstance or accident.

Allow these facts about your baby's brief life to bring you boldness in your grief as well as peace for your soul. I hope you will find incredible healing and peace as you are freed to face the facts about the life you carried. Your baby was the handiwork of God!

As painful as it might be to face your loss at this moment, facing it is the only way to truly begin to heal. As painful as it may be at first, let your heart grieve. Every tear you shed is worthwhile.

With all boldness and love, I encourage you to think of your child as a gift from God. Your baby's life, however brief, was purposed and significant. The Father was and continues to be glorified through your child's precious life. His purpose in that life is being fulfilled even now through you.

PRAYER

Dear God, please help us see our

child as an eternal life that You

created. Hold us tightly, as we

begin to deal with the reality of

our loss. Help us to trust that

You have a plan to make beauty

out of ashes in our lives. Help us

know how to let go and how to

continue on with our lives. Help

us see our child as a gift of life

from You. Amen.

J O U R N A L

What validates the life of your baby for you? There are many evidences that serve as proof that you experienced life within. List some of the things that validate the existence of your baby's life to you (e.g., a pregnancy test, cards, gifts, a heartbeat, sonogram pictures, kicks, stretch marks). How has your baby's brief time here left its imprint on you and your family's hearts and lives?

_____

_____

_____

_____

_____

_____

_____

_____

_____

_____

_____

Glory Baby

Words and Music by Watermark

Glory baby, you slipped away as fast as we could say baby, baby
You were growing, what happened, dear?
You disappeared on us baby, baby
Heaven will hold you before we do
Heaven will keep you safe until we're home with you
Until we're home with you

Chorus:
Miss you every day
Miss you in every way
But we know there's a day when we will hold you
We will hold you
You'll kiss our tears away
When we're home to stay
Can't wait for the day when we will see you
We will see you
But baby let sweet Jesus hold you 'till mom and dad can hold you
You'll just have heaven before we do
You'll just have heaven before we do

Sweet little babies, it's hard to understand it 'cause we're hurting
We are hurting
But there is healing
And we know we're stronger people through the growing
And in knowing—
That all things will work together for our good
And God works His purposes just like He said He would
Just like He said He would

Chorus

I can't imagine heaven's lullabies and what they must sound like
But I'll rest in knowing, that heaven is your home
And it's all you'll ever know
All you'll ever know

Chorus

CHAPTER THREE

FINDING COMFORT AND PEACE

He heals the brokenhearted and binds up their wounds.

PSALM 147:3

It is devastating to lose the treasured life of a baby. In the midst of your loss, it can be difficult to believe that you will ever experience real joy again. To laugh or to smile may seem impossible. But your joy is still there, even though it is masked by your present pain.

Losing a life so new does not seem right. It is *not* the natural order of things. It is *not* the way we always dreamed life would be. Why did we have to say good-bye to our children before we had the opportunity to hold them, love them and watch them grow up?

You may feel the way I did when I looked out my window and saw life continuing unabated—people driving cars, people laughing, children playing—I wanted to scream, "Stop, world! My baby is gone. How can I go on?" Feelings such as these are normal as we cry out in pain for answers that don't seem to be within our grasp. I like the way Mary Jane Worden put it when she wrote, "Sometimes when we ask God our 'Why Questions,' instead of answers He gives us comfort."[1] Her words are so true.

We need to try to accept the mystery of our loss. We don't have to understand it, nor do we have to be able to explain it; we just need to trust that God is in it. God is the only source of true

> *We need to accept the mystery of our loss and trust that God is in it.*

comfort that exists. He knows that your heart is broken and He wants to comfort you.

He has left His Word for each of us. In it we can find verses that specifically address walking through difficult times. His Word can give us strength and encouragement when we feel utterly alone and hopeless. Although at times it can be difficult to see past the pain and loss, you will be amazed at the healing power you can find in His Word.

He gives you peace as you trust in Him:

> You will keep him in perfect peace, whose mind is stayed on You, because he trusts in You (Isa. 26:3, *NKJV*).

The peace He gives surpasses our understanding:

> And the peace of God, which transcends all understanding, will guard your hearts and your minds in Christ Jesus (Phil. 4:7).

He will comfort you during this time so that you will later be able to comfort others with the comfort you have received:

> He is the source of every mercy and the God who comforts us. He comforts us in all our troubles so that we can comfort others. When others are troubled, we will be able to give them the same comfort God has given us (2 Cor. 1:3-4, *NLT*).

He will be with you always:

> He will never leave you nor forsake you (Deut. 31:6).

Allow your heart to be comforted. The peace that He gives goes beyond our understanding. His peace brings rest to our souls when the storms are raging. He will give you a calm that will enable you to continue, despite the circumstances you are walking through. Pray that your eyes will be opened to see Him loving you through the gift of comfort and peace that only He can give. Look for it. It's there.

He might send comfort in the thoughtful gift of a friend or a kind word from a coworker. Perhaps comfort can be found through a friend who provides a few meals for you. Support groups and church groups are a source of comfort for those who experience losses. Books and special songs can speak words of comfort to your heart. The Internet provides access to information that can bring comfort and healing. There are many websites specifically designed for those who have lost a baby through miscarriage, stillbirth or early infant death.[2]

Comfort can be found through time spent with family members. They love you and can give you comfort just by their presence. They will want to know how they can help. Although they may not feel your loss as intensely as you do, they care about you and your pain. Remember that they may be grieving too.

Everyone has their own way of processing loss and grief. Know that there will probably be those, both family members and friends, who cannot relate to your grief and may not understand your pain. Extend grace to them and forgiveness for any well-meaning words that are meant to ease your pain but that actually do the opposite. It is better to express your hurts and give others a chance to explain what they meant to communicate rather than to become angry and bitter. Keep in mind that it is so difficult for others to know the right words to say at a time such as this.

Another great source of comfort comes in knowing someone else who has walked your road or a similar road. I remember that on the day I found out that my baby had died, I wanted to find someone who had been there, too. I longed for someone who could give me even a clue as to what to expect—physically, emotionally and spiritually— in the midst of my storm. I felt as if I were the only one who had ever sailed these waters. I knew that surely this was not the case, but I didn't know where to turn.

I wondered, *Where is God now?* Since He never leaves or forsakes us, where was He during what felt like my darkest moments? It was at that time, as I cried out to God, that I began to truly experience the comfort and peace only He can give. Where was God during my loss? I'll tell you where He was: Looking back now, I see so clearly that He had not forsaken me; He was right there carrying me through the devastation.

He was there in the early weeks of our pregnancy, filling our hearts with joy for the life He created within me. He was there increasing our love and anticipation for a life that would give us a lifetime of memories and love. He was there comforting me as I sat in the doctor's office and saw my baby's lifeless body on the sonogram. He was there giving me a peace I cannot explain as I delivered the tiny, lifeless body of my baby. He was there as we were left with empty arms and broken hearts. He was with us when we told our other children that their little sister would not be joining our family here on Earth. He prompted a couple who personally knew the pain of loss to drop off on our doorstep Dr. Jack Hayford's life-validating and life-giving book *I'll Hold You in Heaven*. God was there comforting me in so many ways and filling me with His peace when I was in the midst of my loss so that today I can share His comfort with you. It is so much easier now, with hindsight, to see how God was there all the time! He was in it all, making beauty out of the ashes in my life. He can do the same for you.

God has comforted me, and He will comfort you—day by day. He understands pain and loss in a personal way and He cares about you. You will be amazed as you walk through one day and then the next and on and on with a peace that surpasses your understanding. You might feel a moment of complete despair and then the next moment you find yourself resting and coping in a peaceful way. Know that God is giving you the comfort and peace you need to sustain you during this time. He will not leave you. He wants to shower you with love and comfort. May you truly experience the hope, comfort and peace that God is waiting to give you every day, moment by moment.

PRAYER

*Dear God, we don't understand the whys,
but help us trust in Your plan. Let us know
Your comfort and peace like never before. Please fill
the emptiness left by our loss. Open our eyes to see
Your goodness again. Comfort us now, as we grieve, so
that someday we will be able to comfort others
who will know this same pain. Amen.*

JOURNAL

From time to time your mind might become flooded with unanswered questions. Know that this is normal. What are some of the things you wonder about? Write them down.

Remember that God is the creator and always creates with purpose. He can handle your why questions. List some of the ways you have found comfort and peace.

_____

_____

_____

_____

_____

_____

_____

_____

_____

_____

_____

_____

PART 2

THE OIL OF GLADNESS
INSTEAD OF MOURNING

His Strength Is Perfect

Words and Music by Steven Curtis Chapman and Jerry Salley

I can do all things
Through Christ who gives me strength
But sometimes I wonder what He can do through me
No glory on my own
Yet in my weakness He is there to let me know

Chorus:
His strength is perfect when our strength is gone
He'll carry us when we can't carry on
Raised in His power, the weak become strong
His strength is perfect, His strength is perfect

We can only know
The power that He holds
When we truly see how deep our weakness goes
His strength in us begins
Where ours comes to an end
He hears our humble cry and proves again

Chorus

GRACE FOR EVERY MOMENT

My grace is sufficient for you, for My strength is made perfect in weakness.

2 CORINTHIANS 12:9, *NKJV*

God promises to give us strength when our strength is gone. When we are weak, He is strong. His Word says that He is close to the broken-hearted (see Ps. 34:18). Don't think that you need to be strong by yourself. You are not alone. God loves you and will be your help. He will carry you through your grief and give you grace for every moment.

During the initial days of my loss, I was amazed at the end of each day that I had made it through. I remember waking up morning after morning feeling desperately sad, defeated and empty. My first few moments of each morning were filled with facing the reality of my loss once again. My emotions were so intense that it was often difficult to function. I felt like I was doing nothing but just making it from one moment to the next. Yet I was surviving when I had thought I wouldn't be able to go on.

For the first time, I understood in a deeply personal way how God's grace was sufficient for me. I had strength, though I was weak and broken. Looking back, I know that God was matching my moments with the perfect amount of grace. He was carrying me, loving me and giving

I know that God was matching my moments of grief with the perfect amount of grace.

me peace. There is no other explanation for it. I was able to handle sharing the news of our loss with family and friends. Just as my every moment of grief was covered by His grace, He will handle what concerns you today and give you what you need to carry on.

You have walked through so much, yet there will probably be more rough days ahead. Grief seems to be a cyclical experience and has a mind of its own. One moment you might feel that you're doing fine, functioning well and coping with your loss; then the next moment you might find yourself overwhelmed with a torrent of emo-

tion. Moments like these are normal and to be expected. Give yourself permission to grieve and to be comforted with the grace and strength God has waiting for you. Know that you will not be traveling this road alone. God will meet you there.

I want to help you prepare for things that might trigger your cycle of grief and sorrow. These triggers can spark raw emotion that will totally catch you off guard as you try to go about your normal routine. You might hear a special song on the radio or pass a familiar smell or sight that will transport you to a place of deeply felt grief again. These triggers are different for everyone and are not respecters of time or place. Simply being aware of possible triggers can help you to deal with your emotions and assure you that your reactions are normal. The following can be especially difficult days for bereaved parents:

- Your baby's due date
- Your birthday
- Christmas
- Valentine's Day
- Mother's Day
- Father's Day
- Your anniversary

When moments like these come, *and they will,* step toward your grief. Continue to face it.

Experiences like these *do not* mean that something is wrong with you or that you are not healing. Actually the opposite is true. You are grieving in a healthy way by releasing the pain built up inside and choosing to remember. There is such healing in the healthy release of emotions. Denying your pain will not make it go away.

Take a moment to look at the blessings of grace and mercy that God has already showered on you. Think about the timing of everything that has happened and how it has all fallen into place. Happenings that some may call coincidences are actually the handiwork of God and come from His grace and mercy. Think for a moment about how far you have come. Think about all the moments you have made it through. You have probably already been amazed by the strength and peace you have found as you continue to move forward day by day. Rest assured that in the coming days you will continue to find the perfect amount of grace and strength you will need for every moment of your grief. God will never leave you.

Please know that it is okay to find your new "normal" as you take time to deal with your emotions and the reality of your loss. Do not feel as if your daily routine has to be exactly the same as it was before. It's absolutely okay to make changes in your schedule in order to gain the time you need to rest and to heal. If you feel that you cannot handle being with a lot of people—that you cannot handle putting on a happy face—then don't. It is fine to take a step back and to bow out of parties, showers and other gatherings for a time. You don't have to jump back into the fast-paced race of life before feeling strong enough emotionally. Take it slowly, one day at a time.

Trust that God will be the stronghold in your storm, a very present help in trouble and an anchor when the winds of grief blow. He will meet all of your moments with the strength to grieve, the power to heal, the ability to grow and the grace to be forever changed for good because of the precious life that passed through you.

PRAYER

Dear God, thank You for Your grace to handle our most difficult moments. Your strength is what we need. Pour out Your grace more and more, since we know there will be more difficult days ahead. Carry us when we feel that we can't carry on. Please draw us closer to each other as a family and closer to You as we walk through this storm. Amen.

J O U R N A L

It is good sometimes to look back and see how far you've come—it encourages you to continue on. The strength you have found moment by moment, day by day, has been a gift from the Lord. He's been carrying you; He has not left your side.

How has God met your every moment with just the right amount of grace? How has He prepared the way for you?

_____

_____

_____

_____

_____

_____

_____

_____

_____

_____

_____

Blessing in the Thorn

Words and Music by Randy Phillips, Dave Clark and Don Koch
Dedicated to Garwin Dobyns

I read about a man of God
Who gloried in his weakness
And I wish that I could be
More like Him and less like me
Am I to blame for what I'm not
Or is pain the way God teaches me to grow
I need to know

When does the thorn become a blessing
When does the pain become a friend
When does the weakness make me stronger
When does my faith make me whole again
I want to feel His arms around me
In the middle of my raging storm
So that I can see the blessing in the thorn

I've heard it said the strength of Christ
Is perfect in my weakness
And the more that I go through
The more I prove the promise true
His love will go to any length
And reaches even now to where I am
But tell me once again

Lord, I have to ask You
On the cross You suffered through
Was there a time You ever doubted
What You already knew

CHAPTER FIVE

GROWING THROUGH THE PAIN

We know that all things work together for good.

ROMANS 8:28, *KJV*

It was never God's desire or His original plan for our lives to be filled with pain. But the fact that we live in a broken, imperfect world and are members of a fallen race continually manifests itself in the forms of sickness, sin, natural disasters, tragedy and death. There's no way around it: Death and pain are a part of life. God has promised, however, never to give us more than we can bear. Only He can take all of our pain and sorrow and work it together for good in our lives.

With every challenge or difficulty that comes our way, we have two choices: to grow through the experience and be forever changed, or let it cripple us and become bitter in the process. No matter how difficult or tragic the circumstance, God can ultimately redeem it and use it for our good. Will you let Him do that now in the midst of your grief?

Words cannot adequately express the pain you have experienced. You are in a place where you never imagined you would ever be. The reality is so difficult to process. It's hard to let go of the hopes and dreams you held for a life so loved and wanted. Even if you only knew of your little one's existence for a short time, you had already grown in your love and anticipation for this treasured life.

Your entire life has been filtered through God's fingers of love. Nothing comes into your life that He cannot handle.

You may be wondering, *How long will it take until I'm over losing my baby?* My answer is that you never have to get over it, in the sense of forgetting the loss. God can comfort and ease your pain, and in time, the pain will be much less intense. But you *never* have to feel that you must get over it because enough time has passed. You want your child's life, however briefly he or she was here, to have its impact on your life. If you

run from your pain, it will not produce the fruit in your life that it could.

God loves you. Even though He didn't cause your pain to happen, He will never leave you nor forsake you in the midst of it. Your entire life has been filtered through His fingers of love. Nothing comes into your life that He cannot handle. He mercifully supplies the grace and strength you need to make it through. Mountaintop experiences are wonderful, but they do not strengthen you in the way that walking through a valley does. It is during the valley experiences, when trials come and you are faced with tough questions, that you truly grow the most. Although this growth can be excruciating, God has promised that He will never permit you to experience more than you can bear. And remember, He is with you!

As you grieve, you will find that time becomes your friend and gradually, day by day, eases the sting of your loss. I have found the old saying Time heals all wounds to be so true. Time gives us the opportunity to work through our pain and to grow in the process. I hope that you will one day look back, as I have been able to do, and see what growth has taken place from walking through your loss. Your heart *will* heal in time.

Time will also help you learn to let go of your need to understand and to have a better closure. Letting go will allow your heart to begin to accept your loss and avoid the trap of bitterness. Letting go releases your heart to go on, but it *doesn't* mean you will forget a life that has left you forever changed.

There are so many ways you can continue to grow as God works your pain and loss together for good:

- You can grow to have a greater appreciation for life and for each day you spend with those you love.
- You can better understand that we are not assured a tomorrow together. That knowledge alone helps you cherish each moment you have with those you love.
- You can commit to praying for others who are expecting a child, because you now have a greater understanding of the fragility of life.
- You can grow in your faith as you learn to rely not on your own strength but on God's strength.
- You can learn to trust that you are a part of a greater plan and that God loves you and is in control.
- You can certainly grow in compassion for others who experience the pain of loss, and you can comfort them with the comfort you have received.
- You are now much better prepared to reach out to others who suffer a loss, and you will know what will be a help to them.

There are untold benefits yet to be discovered as you continue to work though your loss. Allow God to give you a clearer vision of the purpose behind your pain, and look for the blessings among the thorns. George Matheson penned these words that are so fitting:

Dear God, I have never thanked you for my thorns. I have thanked you a thousand times for my roses but never once for my thorns. Teach me the glory of the cross I bear; teach me the value of my thorns. Show me that I have climbed closer to you along the path of pain. Show me that through my tears, the colors of your rainbow look much more brilliant.[1]

PRAYER

Dear God, continue to mold us and make us into the people You desire us to be. Let us grow through our pain rather than become bitter because of it. Help us to find our new "normal." Show us, day by day, the purpose behind our pain. On those days that we can't see past our pain, be strong in us. Let us see how You are working our loss and pain together for good in our lives and in the lives of others who are touched by our loss. Amen.

JOURNAL

Keep in mind that pain, suffering and death were not part of God's original plan. We live in a fallen world where loss is a part of life. As painful as that is, we can grow in the process.

List some of the ways you and others have grown through the pain of your loss and have found the blessings in the thorns. How are you different today?

_____

_____

_____

_____

_____

_____

_____

_____

_____

_____

_____

WITH HOPE

WORDS AND MUSIC BY STEVEN CURTIS CHAPMAN

This is not at all how
We thought it was supposed to be
We had so many plans for you
We had so many dreams
And now you are gone away
And left us with the memories of your smile
And nothing we can say
And nothing we can do
Can take away the pain
The pain of losing you, but

Chorus:
We can cry with hope
We can say goodbye with hope
'Cause we know our goodbye is not the end, oh no
And we can grieve with hope
'Cause we believe with hope
(There's a place by God's grace)
There's a place where we'll see your face again
We'll see your face again

And never have I known
Anything so hard to understand
And never have I questioned more
The wisdom of God's plan
But through the cloud of tears
I see the Father's smile and say well done
And I imagine you
Where you wanted most to be
Seeing all your dreams come true
'Cause now you're home
And now you're free, and

We have this hope as an anchor
'Cause we believe that everything
God promised us is true, so
We wait with hope
We ache with hope
We hold on with hope
We let go with hope

CHAPTER SIX

GRASPING THE HOPE

*In his great mercy he has given us new birth into
a living hope . . . kept in heaven for you.*

1 PETER 1:3-4

What keeps you going from day to day? In the middle of a seemingly hopeless situation, the outcome of which you cannot change, where can you find hope?

Hope is essential to our survival as humans. We live for the hope of a brighter tomorrow, the hope of healing and finding the motivation to live past today. I'm not talking about a wishing-upon-a-lucky-star kind of hope—the kind the world offers. I'm referring to the hope that promises that even the most tragic situations can be redeemed for good. This hope whispers to you that there is someone who can heal your broken heart and bind up your wounds.[1] Hope also assures you of a reunion someday in heaven with your little one. As parents, what greater hope could we desire?

The Bible describes *a living hope* that puts the pain and trials in our lives into perspective and helps us find hope beyond our suffering. In 1 Peter 1:6-7, we read that for a little while we may suffer grief in all kinds of trials, but these have come so that our faith may be proved genuine and may result in praise, glory and honor. God can use our suffering to build our character and to increase our faith. In 2 Samuel 12:13-23, we read about David's son who died shortly

Your time apart from your child who is now in heaven is a temporary situation.

after birth. When his son became ill, David was deeply saddened and pleaded for the Lord to heal him. When David saw that it was not in God's plan to work a miracle to keep his son alive, he got up, dressed and went out to worship God. He knew that his son was with the Lord. David took great comfort in heaven and declared that his child would not return to him, but he would one day go to his child. David had great confidence in the fact that one day he and his child would be reunited in heaven.

For reasons you and I may never understand, God chose not to spare David, you or me from the pain of losing a child. At the time of my own loss, I could not imagine that good could come from such terrible pain. I literally cried out to God on my knees the day of my loss and said, "Prove to me that You can make something good out of the loss of my baby." I couldn't fathom how good could come from the loss of an innocent, wanted baby. But I chose to trust in the Scriptures that had never failed me. I chose to trust in what I knew to be true about God's character. Slowly, day by day, I began to see pieces of God's plan unfold in my life and I grasped more and more the hope of my future in heaven.

There is no greater hope I can offer you than the hope that one day, when your life on Earth is over, you can be reunited with your child. You don't have to grieve like those who have no hope! Hope is what keeps you going when going on means a lifetime of separation from your child. I want to share this hope with you because ignorance forfeits hope. I want to help you put your pain into perspective and find hope beyond your suffering.

From what authority do I say this kind of hope is possible? Through a personal relationship with Jesus Christ, who promises us an eternity in heaven with Him when we know Him as

Savior and Lord! The Bible says, "Believe in the Lord Jesus, and you will be saved" (Acts 16:31). It also says, "No one comes to the Father except through [Christ]" (John 14:6). A relationship with Christ is not a mysterious thing. It is begun through a simple step of faith: believing and receiving Jesus as Lord of your life. John 3:16 says, "Whoever believes in [Jesus] shall not perish but have eternal life." If you do not have assurance in your heart that your eternal home is in heaven, please pray to receive Christ today. You simply need to recognize your need of a Savior. He paid the price to save you when He died on the cross for you. Place your faith and trust in Him, and let Him be the Lord of your life.

When you make a decision to begin a relationship with Jesus, you immediately receive the gift of eternal life in heaven, which can never be taken from you. You can now look forward, with great anticipation, to a future in heaven with your child. C. S. Lewis left us with a beautiful word picture that says our brief lives here on Earth are only the cover to the title page in the novel of our eternal stories that will be lived out to completion in heaven.[2] If you can grasp the reality of this hope for you and for your child, then your pain and loss can be transformed into gladness and hope.

In no way do I want to downplay your grief. On this side of heaven, we will never fully understand why pain and suffering have to come into our lives; but we can rest assured that God will use our suffering to mold and shape us. God is able, if we allow Him, to redeem and transform how we think about what has happened to us. He is the only One who can replace our despair with hope. The Bible says that God is the One who heals the brokenhearted and binds up their wounds (see Ps. 147:3).

You can have comfort and hope in knowing that

- your baby is in perfect peace and will never know pain, sickness, sadness or loss but only joy, peace and eternal happiness (what a thought!);
- God and His angels will hold your little one until Mom and Dad are there;
- you will have the opportunity to see your child in heaven as a result of choosing to invite Jesus Christ into your life as Savior.

I encourage you to embrace your loss from an eternal perspective and see that your time apart from your child who is now in heaven is a temporary situation. In the scheme of eternity, our lives here last but a twinkle of the eye. Rest in the comfort and peace that God wants to give you. Find comfort in knowing that your baby was ushered into the presence of God at the very moment his or her life ceased here on Earth. Instant heaven![3]

PRAYER

Heavenly Father, what hope we can have in You! Fill us with Your hope. Forgive us when we sin against You. Be the Lord of our lives and take control of our days. We need You, Jesus. Thank You for the free gift of eternal life that can be ours for the asking. Please remind us often of the reunion we will have one day in heaven with our little ones because of our faith in You. Thank You for transforming our lives and giving us gladness for mourning. Amen.

If you just made a decision to trust in Christ as your Savior or if you are unsure whether or not you truly have the hope of spending an eternity in heaven with your child, please call 1-888-Need-Him. Someone is waiting there to talk to you about your personal relationship with Jesus Christ.

JOURNAL

In such a seemingly hopeless situation of loss, you can still experience hope! Just like King David, you cannot bring your child back, but you can go to your child one day. That doesn't mean you won't hurt anymore while you're here on Earth, but it does mean that you can have the sure hope of someday joining your child in heaven and then spending eternity together with God. Does that excite you? Encourage you? Describe how belief in an eternal perspective of your loss can increasingly transform your grief.

_____

_____

_____

_____

_____

_____

_____

_____

_____

_____

_____

_____

PART 3

A Garment of Praise, Instead of Despair

Jesus Will Still Be There

WORDS BY ROBERT STERLING
MUSIC BY JOHN MANDEVILLE

Things change
Plans fail
You look for love on a grander scale
Storms rise
Hopes fade
And you place your bets on another day
When the going gets tough
When the ride's too rough
When you're just not sure enough

Chorus:
Jesus will still be there
His love will never change
Sure as the steady rain
Jesus will still be there
When no one else is true
He'll still be loving you
When it looks like you've lost it all
And you haven't got a prayer
Jesus will still be there

Time flies
Hearts turn
A little bit wiser from lessons learned
But sometimes
Weakness wins
And you lose your foothold once again
When the going gets tough
When the ride's too rough
When you're just not sure enough

Repeat chorus twice

When it looks like you've lost it all
And you haven't got a prayer
Jesus will still be there

CHOOSING TO REMEMBER

I thank my God every time I remember you.

P H I L I P P I A N S   1 : 3

When my husband and I experienced our loss, we both longed to find ways to remember and honor the brief life of our little one who touched our hearts in such significant ways. We knew that some people might never understand our need to remember, but we felt sure we were not alone. Through a local support group, we found others who had experienced a treasured life in the womb that softly tiptoed in and out of their lives yet left behind a lifetime of memories and love.

Allow your heart to embrace your memories and the dreams you held for the life of your little one. Cherish anything you have that validates that life. Spend some time thinking about your little one who is now in heaven. Be bold in your grief, and choose to be forever changed by the precious life that passed through yours. Through your memories, you can allow your baby's life to continue to impact others.

Thank God for each remembrance of the life you carried within. Each day was a gift from God. It may be difficult initially to cultivate those memories, but they validate a treasured

Through your memories, you can allow your baby's life to continue to impact others.

life. Choosing to remember the purposed, God-breathed life of your own little one brings sanctity and dignity to *all* life, born or unborn.

One of the ways you can choose to remember is to tell others about the love you hold in your heart for this child. It's okay to mention that one of your children is with the Lord. If you have other children, tell them about their sibling whom they can one day see in heaven. Allowing your children to experience a connection to your baby can give them a greater appreciation for new life. They will also benefit from seeing how

much you care for a life too brief and know that you loved them even before they were born. Just imagine the great anticipation they will have in knowing that one day they will see their brother or sister in heaven.

I encourage you to name your child, if you haven't already done so. Although your baby's life was brief, giving a name to your child will help you think of him or her as a unique individual. If you don't know your baby's gender, don't worry, you can choose a special, endearing term to refer to your baby, such as Baby Smith, Joy, Hope, Punkin', Sweetie. Giving your baby a name allows you to connect with your child on a more personal level and honors that treasured life.

There are so many ways to treasure your memories. Take a moment to look through the checklist of ideas below and choose a few, or come up with some creative ideas of your own. Your family can continue to remember your child's eternal life now perfect and complete in heaven.

· Make or purchase a special box to hold all the treasured things that remind you of your baby (e.g., pregnancy test stick, sonogram pictures, congratulation cards and letters, lock of hair). For years to come, you can visit your treasure box at special times when you want to sit and think about your child.

- Make or purchase a memory keepsake book in which you place mementos of your baby.
- Write letters to your baby. Tell your child all the things you would say if your little one were still here. It is so healing to just put into words the feelings and emotions you carry for this little life.
- Write a message to your baby on a helium-filled balloon. Have a moment of silence to remember and then let it go. Watch it float toward heaven.
- Attend a memory walk or a memorial service held annually by various loss support groups.
- Choose a special stuffed animal that will be a reminder of your baby—something tangible to hold and to cherish.
- Purchase a birthstone ring, necklace or charm that represents the month you lost your baby. It will serve as a precious reminder of how that life touched yours and how you choose to remember.
- Choose and personalize a "Little Footprints" memory keepsake made by Angels in Heaven Ministries (see Resources section of this book).
- Choose a special ornament that will be placed on your Christmas tree each year in honor of your baby. You might even want to begin a family tradition of hanging that special ornament first.
- At Christmastime, purchase a gift for an "angel" from one of the many Angel Trees, and give it "In Memory of (your child's name)". Choose a child who is the age your child would have been. What a blessing it will be for you and the child who receives the gift.

PRAYER

Dear Lord, help us as we choose to remember our little one. Give us more and more boldness in a world that places little value on life in the womb. Help us to see our time with our baby as a gift. Although it hurts so much to let this precious one go and although to our minds the time we had together was far too short, let us never forget the life You created as perfect and purposed by You. Amen.

JOURNAL

A significant creation of God has passed through your life and has left you forever changed. Your little one's presence was known, felt and loved. How will you choose to remember this life that has touched yours forever? Write down some things you have done or would like to do in memory of your baby's brief life as you make a conscious choice to honor a life worth remembering.

_____

_____

_____

_____

_____

_____

_____

_____

_____

_____

_____

_____

VISITOR FROM HEAVEN

WORDS AND MUSIC BY TWILA PARIS

A visitor from heaven
If only for awhile
A gift of love to be returned
We think of you and smile

A visitor from heaven
Accompanied by grace
Reminding of a better love
And of a better place

With aching hearts and empty arms
We send you with a name
It hurts so much to let you go
But we're so glad you came
We're so glad you came

A visitor from heaven
If only for a day
We thank Him for the time He gave
And now it's time to say
We trust you to the Father's love
And to His tender care
Held in the everlasting arms
And we're so glad you're there
We're so glad you're there

With breaking hearts and open hands
We send you with a name
It hurts so much to let you go
But we're so glad you came
We're so glad you came

CHAPTER EIGHT

COMMUNICATING YOUR HEART

Be of good courage, and He shall strengthen your heart, all you who hope in the LORD.

PSALM 31:24, *NKJV*

How are you supposed to handle the shocking news that something is wrong with your baby? Do you allow yourself to fall apart, or do you pretend and put up a front that you are strong and can handle it? If you have already suffered the loss of your precious baby, how do you think you should appear in front of others?

You don't have to be strong for everyone else. It's okay to let others know how you feel. You may initially want to spend more time alone rather than have lots of people around, or you may feel more comfortable surrounded by family and friends. Just do what you need to do to make it through your initial moments of loss. There is no right or wrong way. If you feel a need to talk about your loss, please do. It's fine to tell anyone with whom you are talking that you need them to listen but not give you answers. It's okay to feel numb, hurt, angry and overwhelmingly sad. You are human, and you hurt. You don't have to put on a show for others. Those who love you and care about you will want to know your heart.

You have a significant story to tell. Be bold about sharing your heart.

It is very important to learn to communicate what you are feeling inside. Keeping your feelings bottled up will only cause you more pain and alienate you from those who love you. It may not be your personality to be open with your feelings, but you can still learn to at least admit that you're sad. When someone asks if you're okay, you can say "No, not really," if that's how you're feeling. Be honest with yourself and with others. As time passes, it will become easier to share what you feel.

The day of our loss, I remember my husband saying, "Man, I wish I had known how much the guy at our office was hurting when he casually mentioned that he and his wife had a pregnancy loss this year." He continued, "I didn't know what to say or how to act. Now I want to go back to him and listen a little more closely and intently and tell him that I'm very sorry." For the first

time, we began to understand in a personal way the importance of acknowledging life in the womb as treasured and significant, no matter how brief that life was.

If you have other children, they are experiencing the pain of loss, too. Just like you, they had hopes and dreams for the baby. I remember feeling so surprised at how brokenhearted my three-year-old and four-year-old were when they learned that our baby would not be joining our family here on Earth. They had a great need to talk about their loss. It was good to cry together and talk about how important each member of a family is. This can be a wonderful opportunity to talk to your children about the preciousness of each life, because God created it. Encourage your children to communicate their hearts. Don't be surprised if they want to tell their friends and others that one of their family members is in heaven. If we could only be as honest and bold as children!

When I began speaking of my loss, I was surprised at how many of our own family and friends came forward with stories of their own losses. Why hadn't I heard about them before? Why are so many parents silent about the life that for a few days, weeks or months brought such joy and promise? How many times do we want to share our story, but we close up and keep it hidden for fear of rejection or being thought of as weird? It happens too often—but especially if the loss was during early pregnancy.

As I continued to heal from my loss and talk about it, I would mention in casual conversation my need to remember our little one. This seemed to open wide the door of communication with others who had endured a similar loss. Many times, a floodgate of emotion that had been bottled up inside the person for years—sometimes as long as 20 or 30 years—would pour out. You have a significant story to tell. Be bold about sharing your heart with family and friends. Talking about your loss and the good you have seen come from it can be healing for yourself and others. When you begin to talk to people, you may find that you're the only one who has ever taken the time to hear their story.

Accept the freedom to say "I have (number) children here and (number) in heaven." Our children in heaven should be remembered and honored on Mother's Day, Father's Day and on Sanctity of Human Life Day. Are these lives any less significant than those we try to save through the pro-life movement? Absolutely not! Is God a respecter of persons? No! All of His creations are valued by Him and should be valued by us, too.

I encourage you to share your story with others, especially with those who, like you, have experienced a loss. Give yourself permission to communicate your heart and let others continue to be touched by the life that passed through you. The more you share, the more comfortable you will feel about sharing, and you will see your little one's brief life bless others.

PRAYER

Dear Lord, help me to communicate with others the hope I hold in my heart. Give me grace and guard my heart from well-meaning family and friends whose words sometimes hurt more than help. Help me to take this experience of loss and grow from it. Let me know what it is to be comforted by You, so then, out of that comfort, I can comfort others. Let me be changed for good because of a life that has impacted mine for eternity.

JOURNAL

I encourage you to look at your life and to see how you have become equipped to help and comfort others because of the help and comfort you have received. Look for opportunities to see how your baby's life can continue to touch others through you.

What are some of the things people have done and said that have been helpful and healing for you?

How has your experience of loss affected the way you will now treat others who experience the loss of a treasured life?

How are you now better equipped to reach out and comfort others who experience the loss of a treasured life?

_____

_____

_____

_____

_____

_____

_____

_____

My Life Is in Your Hands

Words and Music by Kathy Troccoli and Bill Montvilo

Life can be so good
Life can be so hard
Never knowing what each day
Will bring to where You are
Sometimes I forget
Sometimes I can't see
That whatever comes my way
You'll be with me

Chorus:
My life is in your hands
My heart is in your keeping
I'm never without hope
Not when my future is with You
My life is in Your hands
And though I may not see clearly
I will lift my voice and sing
Your love does amazing things
Lord I know
My life is in your hands

Nothing is for sure
Nothing is for keeps
All I know is that Your love
Will live eternally
So I will find my rest
And I will find my peace
Knowing that
You'll meet my every need

Chorus

When I'm at my weakest
Oh You'll carry me
Then I become my strongest
Lord in Your hands

CHAPTER NINE

CONTINUING ON

For I know the plans I have for you, . . . plans to prosper you and not to harm you, plans to give you hope and a future.

JEREMIAH 29:11

Each of us, from the very beginning of our existence, was designed and created with purpose, to have a hope and a future. My prayer is that the freshness of your pain will heal in a healthy way and you will find the strength that God offers you. Although you and I probably would want to change everything in a moment if we could, God has a plan for our children and for us. He has a hope and a future planned for them that will be lived out in a glorious place with no sorrow, no pain and no tears. Your little one will just have heaven that much sooner than you. Let these truths encourage your heart as you look ahead with hope to the future.

What now? You may or may not want to try again for another child. This is a very personal decision between you and your spouse. Or you may, as I did, have a strong desire to be pregnant again soon after your loss.

God began to fill with hope and peace the void left by the absence of my baby.

I remember that my mind would fluctuate between longing for the baby I had lost and wanting to be pregnant again, though I would feel guilty for even considering moving on. Although I had such a feeling of urgency to experience again the hopeful feelings of pregnancy, I knew that no child would ever replace the one I had lost.

There was also the fear of another loss. I wondered how I would ever again be able to open my heart to having another child. In my mind I walked through various scenarios of wanting to stay detached from emotion with the next pregnancy and wanting to keep it absolutely secret for as long as I could. I was sure that I wouldn't tell a soul until I was very far along, thinking that would somehow protect me from the pain of another loss. What I didn't realize was that I would need friends who loved me to support me through whatever would come.

You may be experiencing some of the same thoughts and emotions. I have found this to be a very common thread among parents who have suffered a loss. Take time to process your loss and to heal both physically and emotionally before making a decision to continue growing your family. As I thought through what I was feeling, God began to fill with hope and peace the void left by the absence of my baby. I slowly began to let go and trust my heart to love again.

As much as I would like to tell you differently, in this imperfect world there are no guarantees of having a healthy, full-term pregnancy the next time you try. What we forget is that this is true of each and every pregnancy, because conception itself is a miracle and life in the womb is fragile. This is where trust comes in. God has a plan for each life He creates. Remember how Psalm 139 says that He knew us before any of our days came to be (see v. 16). He is the only one who holds the key to life. He will create when it is His plan to do so. You're not just taking a chance if, after a time, you decide to open your hearts to another pregnancy.

You will go on. For a while you will just go through the motions: getting up, going to work, washing, cooking, cleaning—day after day. Then one day you will realize that you have made it to the other side. In time, you will learn to let go of your need to understand, your need for better closure and your frustration toward others who can't fully understand how you feel. Psalm 116:9 says that you will again walk "in the land of the living." Life won't just stop, although for a while it may seem like it. You will live again, smile again, laugh again. You will find joy and purpose again, as you grow through your loss and become a better person for having walked through this difficult time.

PRAYER

Dear Lord, as I walk on, let me never forget. Though my child and I are apart,
let my memories live in my heart. Let me see light where there is darkness.
Please help me to heal fully. Amen.

JOURNAL

You have come a long way in your grief. Life didn't stop at the moment of your loss, although you may have wanted it to. Life kept going, and so have you! You are making it—step by step, hour by hour and day by day. Remember that God heals the broken-hearted and binds up their wounds.

Where are you finding strength to continue on? In what are you placing your hope for a brighter tomorrow? Describe how you have grown. What does "continuing on" mean to you?

_____

_____

_____

_____

_____

_____

_____

_____

_____

_____

_____

PART 4

STORIES OF LOSS, HEALING AND HOPE

Julia's Story

Debbie Heydrick

In May of 1994, while my husband, Doug, was on a business trip, I found out that we were expecting our fourth child. It was a few days before Father's Day and I wanted to be creative with the announcement. I decided to send Doug flowers and have them delivered to his meeting. I chose four roses: three that had begun to bloom and one that was still an unopened bud. The note that accompanied the flowers read "Happy Father's Day from all of your children. You'll find a rose from each child."

Doug called me after receiving the flowers and told me they were beautiful and he was touched. He then mentioned that the florist had made a mistake by putting an extra bud in the arrangement. I was silent for a moment and then said, "That was no mistake." After a few moments, Doug said, "Four children? Are we expecting?" What a priceless moment! It will always be in my memory. I could actually feel Doug's joy through the phone line. We were so excited that we didn't want to hang up the phone that night.

A few days later, when he returned home from his trip, he came in with newborn baby diapers, chocolates and a congratulations card. He said, "I just know that God has another little girl for our family. I already have a name chosen for her—Julia!" What excitement filled our hearts as we began to dream together about our growing family!

I decided that since this was our fourth child, I didn't need to be in a great hurry to see a doctor. I began taking prenatal vitamins and scheduled my appointment many weeks out. We began to announce to family and friends about our Valentine's Day gift to come. How perfect that our baby was due on Valentine's Day! We would have a priceless gift: a new child to love and hold.

As the weeks passed, our anticipation to know this child grew. We would talk and sing to the baby, as we had done with all our children. Soon I outgrew my jeans and transitioned into maternity clothes. I was so very surprised how quickly I popped out and began to show with this fourth pregnancy. It was such a joyful time for our family.

At the end of July, Doug accompanied me when I went in for a routine sonogram. As the parents of three children, we were giggling under our breath at the young green couples sitting in the waiting room at the OB-GYN office, waiting to have their pregnancies confirmed. After quite a wait, we jumped up when our names were called for the sonogram.

The technician was so nice and asked us lots of questions about our other children. She began the sonogram and looked at the screen intently while scanning my belly. Then she said, "Tell me again the date of your last period. Could your dates be off by a bit?" I quickly said that I was sure about the conception date because my cycle was very regular. I told her that I was 10 weeks along and already could notice the growth of my belly. After a few more moments of silence, she asked if she could step out of the room for a moment and speak to my doctor. The doctor came in and took a look at the scan and said that things did not look right. He could find the baby but couldn't detect a heartbeat. I was hoping that he would keep looking until his findings changed. The doctor soon put down the transducer and asked me to dress and meet him in his office. I had never before felt so panicky, so empty, so unable to control my world than at that moment. Doug was there with me and we couldn't even speak.

Never in my mind had I imagined that one of my little ones might not make it into my arms. The emotions that flooded my heart and my mind were indescribable. Surely when we walked into the doctor's office to talk, he would give us some hope. We must have misunderstood what had just happened. We were having a baby. Nothing could be wrong. *We were having a baby!*

The doctor's words were so painful to hear. He asked me if I was cramping or had experienced any bleeding. I quickly told him with confidence, "No, everything has been fine!" I was sure this would make a difference in the report he gave us. He would tell us to go home and come back in a few more days and we would be able to see the baby's heartbeat. That was not what the doctor said at all. He told us that our baby was there in body, but its life was gone and we were experiencing a miscarriage. I couldn't even process those words. The pain of facing this loss felt too overwhelming. I asked if I could have another sonogram. I felt in my heart that a higher-level scan would provide different results. After all, I had been growing; I felt tired; and I had so many hopes and plans for this precious life within me.

We scheduled another sonogram. This one gave us the same results, and I was told that I could either take care of things quickly and be done or I could sentence myself to being a walking casket for days or perhaps even weeks before I lost the baby naturally. He warned me that the natural route would be inconvenient, painful and unnecessary. I tried to process all he said, but I felt in my heart that I needed time to face the reality of broken dreams, to process the why of it all and to find closure and say good-bye. Doug and I walked out of that office with heavy hearts. How could this be happening to us? We had always had healthy babies. I didn't even know anyone close to me who had experienced the loss of a baby. How had this happened, and what now?

We left for home and began to grieve and think through how to handle this news. The next several days were a blur. I don't remember much except that I didn't want to volunteer to have the baby taken from my body. If it was my choice, I wanted nature to run its course. I was in great pain emotionally but felt normal physically. I felt pregnant. I *was* pregnant. The next week was long but gave me time to continue on and try to find my new normal as I waited for the moment I would lose the treasured life I still held within me. As painful as it was, this gave me time to process all that had happened.

A little more than a week after we received the news that our baby had died, I awoke during the night to find myself in labor. I was having contractions four minutes apart. By morning I was

bleeding and needed to see my doctor. I was so thankful that Doug was with me. When I finally saw the doctor, he said that I was bleeding too badly and needed to have a D & C. I was disappointed that I had waited so long and been through so much and was still going to need a D & C. As I stood up and walked over to sign papers for surgery, I felt myself beginning to deliver my tiny baby. I was quickly rushed into a room at the doctor's office and delivered.

It was certainly unlike any of my other deliveries. There was no joy or excitement in the air, just a cold metal pan for my baby to drop into and be rushed away to a lab. Looking back, I wish so much that I had asked to see the baby. I felt almost ashamed for wanting to look at her lifeless body, so I didn't ask. At the time, I didn't know that it was an acceptable thing to do. I was in such shock as Doug and I lay, not speaking, in that room. After quite a wait, a nurse came in and said, "You can get dressed now and check out when you are ready. Just make a follow-up appointment and you're free to go." As she left, I thought to myself, *What now? Do we just pretend we know what to do and how to handle this?* That is just what we did. I quickly got dressed and we headed out.

On the way home, we decided to stop by a restaurant to get a bite to eat. After all, we already had a baby-sitter. We were trying to carry on as if nothing had happened. As we sat there in the restaurant, we both began to cry and wonder aloud, "What are we doing? We were pregnant a little while ago and now we are not. What just happened?" Our baby had died and we were acting like nothing had happened. Everything within us cried out that we had just experienced life—a significant life—as it passed through ours. We couldn't sit there any longer and pretend otherwise. We quickly got up, tears pouring from our eyes, packed up our food and headed home.

As soon as we arrived home, Doug put me to bed to rest in our quiet house and said that he needed to go out for a while. He was determined to find something, anything, to remember our baby by. He said that he might be gone awhile but that he wouldn't return without something we could have and hold that would validate our baby's life and help us and our children to remember. I was so touched by his boldness and his declaration of love for our baby. While he was gone, I just wept and cried out to God to show me purpose behind this pain and loss. I screamed, "Prove to me how You can work all this out for good, just like Your Word tells me You will." I was so broken physically, emotionally and spiritually. As I cried out to God, He answered. In those moments of grief, He comforted me and gave me a peace that is indescribable.

I began to think through where we had walked during the past week and a half. Our lives had been turned upside down by this tragedy. I thought about how much it had impacted my thoughts, my emotions, my beliefs and my family. My baby's life certainly wasn't what the world describes as a mere product of conception. This was a life that had left its footprints on my heart—it was a treasured life that had quickly and quietly, almost silently, left us with a lifetime of memories and love.

I was astounded at the impact of my miscarriage. Could I be the only one on Earth who felt this way and saw value in a life that ended short of its entry into this world? Was something wrong with us for caring so deeply for and feeling so greatly affected by a miscarried life? During those first few hours of my loss, as I grieved alone while waiting for Doug to return, I didn't yet know what my desire to remember and my choice to never forget would mean in my life.

A burning desire is the only way I can describe the deep emotion I experienced. I wanted to remember my baby and to think on all the little things that validated the life I had carried within me. My greatest fear was that I might go on with life unchanged. I can remember calling a very special friend who had in every sense of the word been a sister to me for many years. I told her, "Please *never* let me forget about this life.

Please remind me from time to time, and know that you can say something to me about my baby on special days like birthdays, Valentine's Day and Christmas. It's okay to remind me." She had not experienced this kind of loss and probably couldn't fully understand what I was trying to communicate; but just the same, I wanted to be accountable to someone always to remember my little one who was now in heaven, waiting for me.

Our culture doesn't recognize life in the womb as valued life, and it was difficult to boldly say those words. For days, weeks, months and years, I have replayed the conversation in my head, asking myself, *Was that stupid to say? Am I weird? Do I have a problem accepting my loss? Was this loss of life really that big a deal?* Then I would always come back to the realization of what I believe: valuable, God-breathed life begins in the womb at the moment of conception; therefore, my loss was that of a life, a baby.

Many hours later, Doug finally returned home. He began to share with me about all the places he had gone but been unable to find anything that validated life in the womb as life worth remembering. He then handed me a tiny box and a card. Before he let me open the card, he said, "I hope you don't mind, but I used the name Julia for our baby." I was touched by his heart and sensitivity, and I would love to say that I wholeheartedly agreed at first; but the truth is,

I said, "Oh, Doug, do we have to waste that name we love for a baby we will never get to have and hold?" At that very moment, I realized I had bought into the lie of the world's system that we are programmed to believe. If I truly believed that my baby's eternal life had value, then a logical step would be to dignify that life with a name. But, oh, how this hurt to actually face my loss in such a real way! Yet it seemed to give a bit of closure that we needed.

Doug began to tear up and replied, "Debbie, that was our baby, and our baby deserves to have a name. That was the name we had chosen for her. Please, let me call her Julia." In a moment that I will never forget, I agreed to wholeheartedly proclaim her brief yet treasured life with a name. I then opened the tiny card that said "This is in loving memory of Julia." The next moment was so precious. I opened the box and saw a simple, beautiful ring with a heart-shaped peridot stone and three tiny little diamonds. The heart-shaped stone was in memory of Julia and signified her entrance to heaven in August of 1994. The tiny diamonds on the side were in honor of our little ones we were still able to physically hold and love. We held the treasured ring and cried together. Then Doug placed it on my finger and we had something permanent to remind us of our Julia.

A few days later, a couple that also had experienced a loss, dropped by our home and gave us a wonderful book entitled *I'll Hold You in Heaven* by Dr. Jack Hayford. Through this book, our hearts were encouraged and our grief was validated as we began to learn more about the significance of life in the womb. We found incredible encouragement in Dr. Hayford's life-giving words. We were encouraged to find ways to see Julia's life continue to change us. We desired for God to work our loss together for good (see Rom. 8:28) and to prove His Scripture true in our lives.

Now that we knew personally the pain of loss, we began to look for opportunities to reach out to other grieving parents. We had new empathy, and God was so faithful to bring others into our lives to whom we could minister.

In June of 1996, a dear friend lost a baby, Hannah, at 17 weeks of pregnancy. We grieved with the family; and out of our desire to comfort them, Doug decided to create a keepsake in honor of Hannah. We put on it a treasured poem, "Little Footprints" by Dorothy Ferguson, that spoke the words of our hearts in a beautiful way, and then we personalized it with Hannah's name and the date of her going home to heaven. We were able to take this keepsake to the hospital at the time of Hannah's delivery, and her little footprints were printed on it. That same day, Doug made a memory keepsake for our family in honor of our little Julia. After these initial keepsakes were created, we began to share similar keepsakes with friends and acquaintances.

Another treasured friend, who knew our heart's desire to comfort others, called me one day with the Scripture from 2 Corinthians 1:3-4 and told me that we were doing just what that Scripture talked about. That verse says that we are to comfort others in their trials with the comfort that we ourselves have received from Christ. Doug and I have been comforted in more ways than we can ever express. That Scripture became our mission statement for the work God was already doing in and through us.

For the past eight years, since the loss of Julia, God has continued to give us many, many opportunities to touch His hurting children with His love. God has honored our hearts by allowing us the privilege of starting a nonprofit ministry, Angels in Heaven Ministries, through which we have shared our memory keepsakes with hurting families around the world. As a result, we have had the opportunity to pour into lives the hope and comfort of Christ.

We praise God for the opportunity to share our little one's brief life with you. It is our prayer that as you continue to heal, you will choose to remember the gift of life that God entrusted to you and that you will look forward to how God will give you beauty for ashes, gladness for mourning and hope for despair.

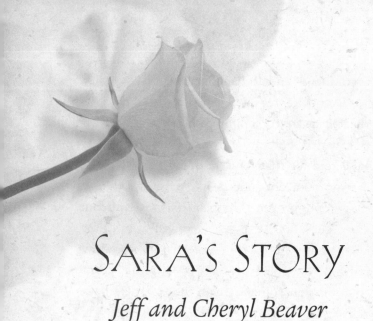

SARA'S STORY

Jeff and Cheryl Beaver

August 24, 1997

Tonight has been a most amazing night, Sara. Amidst our sadness and mourning is peace that could only come from God. Our loss of you is heaven's gain. May the angels rejoice!

It's late on Sunday night, several hours since your mother's miscarriage here at home. Your mother (Cheryl) is asleep, resting after a physically and emotionally draining experience. You, my child, were conceived in love. You are a very real expression of the love your mother and I have for each other. Your mother surprised me in announcing the great news of your pending arrival.

We both have been so excited about the prospect of meeting you. Now we'll look forward to seeing you in heaven. I'll never forget your mother telling me how special she felt you were (and still are). Her comment emphasized the specialness aspect. I wondered often if God had a specific, unique plan for you. Of course He did (and still does). Could this be what Cheryl was sensing?

I will never doubt God's power to create, especially after seeing you. We could see your head, arms and hands forming. The fetal sac was about the size of a quarter and your body was less than an inch long. I hope you know how much I love you. You are here with us as we lay down to sleep tonight.

We will think of you often, my sweet child.

I love you,
Dad

January 31, 1998

Lord, I can't believe it has been five months since you called our little Sara home to heaven. It felt like my heart would break in two the night I miscarried her. The emptiness within me was so painful! At the same time, I was in total awe of the precious little body I saw that was only three-quarters of an inch long.

Thank you for giving me the privilege of seeing our precious baby. Jeff and I are even more passionate about the preciousness of the life of a child from the moment of conception. I longed to feel her growing within me.

I would love to know what she would have looked like and what her personality would have been. I want so badly to be able to express my love to her the way I do to Hope and Austin.

Please, tell her how much I miss her and love her. Tell her of our family's conversations of her and that whether or not she is physically here with us, she will always be an important part of our family. We will love her at a distance with all the passion with which we love each other.

We will not ignore that her life of eight weeks was for a purpose and brought glory to You, Lord. Honoring her has brought peace to my heart in the midst of my grieving.

You have used our other children, Hope (4 years old) and Austin (2 years old), in so many ways to be a part of my healing. I'm so glad we shared this experience with them! Hope is so open about sharing with people that she has a baby sister in heaven. She includes Sara when counting how many are in our family, and when she's praying and thanking the Lord for each person in our family, she always includes Sara. She wants to shop and look at baby clothes, and she comments on what would have looked good on Sara. Her real desire is for us to buy an outfit and mail it to heaven!

Austin is really too young to carry on much conversation about his baby sister, but the most precious thing he does that tells us he understands is when he lets a balloon go to heaven and tells us he's sending it to baby Sara. We gave Austin and Hope little rings with Sara's name and birth date engraved on the inside. Those rings are special to them now, and we pray they will always be a keepsake to remind them of their sister until they get to meet her in heaven.

There is such peace and healing if we will not forget the precious souls that wait for us in heaven. I trust You, Lord, to carry us through this time of grieving, and I thank You for Your never-ending love.

Your mommy

SARA'S SONG

Sometimes I think I hear laughter in my ears.
I smile and hope that she might be very near,
That precious girl we knew such a short time—
Your gift of love, his and mine.

I now can see through the tears and the pain,
Through all the doubt that I'd ever praise Your name.
Yet through the words of a precious friend of mine,
You spoke Your love, Lord, once again.

And now I know there was a reason,
Though I may never understand.
There is no life that is mistaken
And my heart can know the comfort that
You hold her in Your hand.

I look around at the faces that I know.
Some seem afraid, some seem very much alone.
I wish they all could understand
The love that is found in Your plan.

For now I know there is a reason
For all the things that happen here.
And it is only for a season
'Til we see our loving Father and He wipes
our every tear.

So, Lord, please tell her that we love her,
And we're so sad that we're apart.
But we will keep the memory of her,
And until she's in our arms, we will
hold her in our hearts.
Yes, until she's in our arms, we will
hold her in our hearts.

Written by a friend, Rebekah Drury, in honor
of Sara's brief little life.

Baby Reed's Story

Leslie Nunn Reed

Lying on the exam table, I felt the cool gel touch my belly. In seconds my husband and I would hear the first womb sounds of our growing child. The midwife confirmed that at 10½ weeks we should be able to hear the sweet swish, swish of this little one's heartbeat.

Scott and I had been trying to conceive for some months and knew that we were pregnant—having watched and counted the days that would alert us to the conception or the obvious sign that no life had been created. Without much waiting, we shared our good news with family and friends. The congratulations and good wishes poured in each day in notes, calls, cards and e-mails—all saved in a special box. One letter, from my sister, Kristin, was especially tender:

Saturday, May 12, 2001

Baby Reed,

It is your grandma Nunn's birthday. I just got home from dinner with your mom and dad and Grandma and Grandpa Nunn. We had a great time at The Old Warsaw in Dallas. As we presented cards to your grandma after our meal, your mom and dad gave her one announcing you! I cannot tell you how much joy I have right now at the thought of you. Oh, how I have longed for you. I can't wait—in less than 9 months I will be holding you and looking at your body formed by God. I will be smelling your sweet baby scent and hearing your first precious sounds.

I pray you're a cuddly baby who sleeps through the night and doesn't cry a lot. I pray you are healthy in every way and that your mom and dad are healthy and safe. I pray God will prepare them spiritually, mentally and emotionally, and that He would guide and direct them as they prepare your first home for you. I pray you would come to know God at an early age and would desire to walk in His ways all your days. I couldn't stop smiling on the drive home. I have had close friends tell me they were pregnant and I've been thrilled—but my own sister! I can hardly imagine all the wonderful times we will have together. I get to watch you grow in every way. What a privilege.

I look forward to hearing you call me whatever you decide to call me. I can't wait for you to wrap your arms around my neck whenever I come to see you. I'll love when you ask me questions, even 20 in a row. I can't wait for you to come spend the night with me. I just can't wait to see you. I love you. I have loved you since before you were formed. Always remember your significance comes from Christ Jesus and you can do all things through Him.

My love with kisses,
Aunt Kristin

How this child was loved already!

Now, we would hear our baby for the first time. The midwife moved the Doppler probe to another spot on my abdomen. We heard no sounds. The next spot yielded nothing. Based on my size and frame, Kathleen suggested that we have a sonogram the next day, since no technician was immediately available. She reassured us that sometimes 10 weeks can be a little early to hear the heartbeat and that 12 to 14 weeks is more reliable.

We left the office feeling anxious yet trusting in God's provision. The next day we studied the small gray ultrasound screen in the dim room while the technician relayed what she saw—no heartbeat, a sac that measured 10-week size and a fetal pole that measured 6-week size. Our baby had stopped growing a month earlier, but my body hadn't rejected the fetus. The medical community calls this a missed abortion. What a gruesome term.

What followed were decisions about whether or not to pass the fetus naturally or to have a D & C. We spent the rest of the afternoon lying on the bed, praying and holding each other. In the evening we joined my parents and sister for dinner and were comforted with their embraces and tears.

Opting to have a D & C, I recovered quickly—physically. The emotional grieving and healing took much longer. My treasure box of cards is now filled with notes of condolence on the miscarriage. The hardest part may have been not knowing for the longest time that the fetus had died. As I believed that my baby was growing inside, our hopes and desires grew, too. How we loved this little baby. Now we had empty arms and faced many more months before we might welcome another baby into our family.

Ten months later I became pregnant again, though no cards with good wishes came when we announced our second pregnancy. We all seemed to be waiting to see what might happen. Sometimes it was hard to feel joy. Now, seven months pregnant, I feel more confident and am so excited about welcoming this child.

Oddly, when people ask if this is our first child, I respond, "Yes, it is," recognizing that what they're really asking is if we have more children at home. To say "Well, we had a miscarriage last year" or "Our first baby died" immediately puts a damper on the conversation. They want to respond with sensitivity and compassion for our loss. The joyous moment for this new baby is gone.

In this past year, God has brought us comfort and the capacity to grieve with other couples who have experienced a similar loss. These couples are all around us—I never knew. My eyes and heart have been opened. I pray that God will continue to lead me into the lives of others and that I will be available to share their sorrow. It is in this sharing and carrying of one another's burdens that we fulfill the ministry of Jesus.

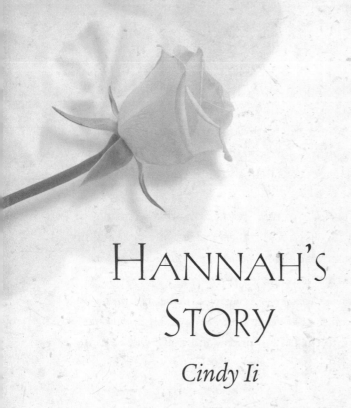

HANNAH'S STORY

Cindy Ii

When I think back on the loss of my little girl Hannah, the thought that comes to mind often is, *She would be turning six years old.* As I sat in church last Sunday and watched the little girl in the pew in front of me, I kept thinking, *I could have had a little girl sitting next to me just like her.* It is such a deep pain and sorrow that one experiences in the loss of a child, whether during a pregnancy or after. God gives us such an amazing love for our children, and it is difficult to understand how a little person that we have known such a short time can take such a hold of our heart.

When I found out at the doctor's office on May 30 that my baby's heartbeat had stopped, I wondered why. I had hoped to find out a reason when she was delivered four days later. The doctor could not give me any definite reason. I ultimately knew that it didn't matter what the cause of her death was, because my husband, Ken, and I believe in a sovereign God and we knew Hannah never belonged to us to begin with.

The pain of her loss was experienced through our whole family. My daughter Rebekah was with me at the doctor's appointment when we could not find the baby's heartbeat, and then she was with me when we did the ultrasound and saw Hannah's still little body inside me. All four of my children understood the pain the weekend I carried her before delivering on June 3. My son Jeremiah, who was eight years old at the time, prayed the whole weekend that the ultrasound would be wrong and that Hannah would still be alive come Monday morning when she was to be delivered. On that Monday, God was merciful and gave me a quick labor and delivery, with no complications. Ken brought our four children to see their little sister. My son Josiah was 13 years old, Rebekah was 10 years old, Jeremiah was 8 years old, and Sarah was turning 6 years old. They all held her in their arms and witnessed how perfect life is from very early in a pregnancy.

All six of us only saw and held her for a few minutes, but she has left an imprint on each of our hearts for a lifetime.

Both of my daughters have written about Hannah. Sarah was only 6 years old when we lost Hannah, but the memory and love is still with her. She wrote the poem "A Sister I Will Always Love" in September 2002, when she was 12 years old.

A Sister I Will Always Love

*One day my dad got our family together in
the living room.
We did not know why.
Then he said the words I will never forget,
He said your mom is going to have a baby.
We were very excited.
My mom was working that night, so we got
her a card and some snacks.
We took them to her at her work.
We told her we would help her around the house.
We told her we would be kind and good to each other.
And we told her we were happy that a
new baby was coming.
Life could not have been happier for me.
Several weeks later my mom had a
doctor's appointment.
My older sister Rebekah had never heard the baby's
heartbeat so she went with my mom.
The doctor tried to find the heartbeat but could not.
He said let's go do a sonogram of the baby.
They took a look at the baby, and the doctor said*

*the baby was not moving and the heartbeat
was not beating.
My mom started crying and my sister Rebekah did too.
They knew that the baby had died.
We were very sad.
I know God had a plan for her in heaven.
We decided to name her Hannah.
She was God's gift to us for a short while.
My mom had to deliver Hannah.
She went to the hospital.
And after she was delivered, my daddy
took us to see her.
I still remember holding her.
She was so tiny and so fragile.
She was the size of my daddy's palm.
I try to imagine what it would be like
if she had not died.
It would be very different with a six-year-old sister.
She was so tiny, she was so young, and she
was not yet born,
And she will always be the sister I love.*

Joel David's Story

Ike and Dana Patrick

My husband and I were expecting our first baby. We were so excited! I found out in July of 1996, when I was about four weeks along, that our baby was to arrive around April 3, 1997. At the time, I was working the evening shift at a nearby hospital and began to have some bleeding. We went to see my doctor the next day and were told that it was early in the pregnancy but there was a possibility that I might be carrying twins based on where the bleeding was coming from. We would have to wait and see.

I continued to work. After a long shift one day, nine weeks into the pregnancy, I went home and started to have some heavy bleeding. The next morning an ultrasound showed that there was only one baby with a strong heartbeat. I was encouraged to quit my job and take it easy, so I did.

We continued to get ready for our little arrival. We had found a home to buy and had our closing set for November 7, 1996. On November 5, my water broke early in the morning, sending me to labor and delivery. I was almost 20 weeks along in my pregnancy. The doctor on call met us at the hospital, and after confirming my worst fear, proceeded to tell us that our baby would not survive the delivery. At 20 weeks, our baby had not yet developed enough lung capacity to breathe outside the womb. Somehow I managed to request a sonogram, so I could see my baby alive one more time before I delivered him. On the sonogram we could see him still moving, but as a pediatric nurse, I could tell that his heart rate had already begun to slow down.

My doctor came in and began to induce labor. He told us that we would be able to hold the baby for as long as we wanted. After about two hours of labor, I delivered a tiny baby boy—perfectly formed in every way. He weighed only 10 ounces and was 8 inches long. He looked like his daddy. I was reminded of Psalm 139:13-16 *(NASB)*:

For You formed my inward parts; You wove me in my mother's womb. I will give thanks to You, for I am fearfully and wonderfully made [He was! He was so perfect!]; wonderful are Your works, and my soul knows it very well. My frame was not hidden from You, when I was made in secret, and skillfully wrought in the depths of the earth; Your eyes have seen my unformed substance; and in Your book were all written the days that were ordained for me [20 weeks in my womb], when as yet there was not one of them.

This passage became so real to me as I held my baby boy. His heart was still beating when they handed him to me. We named him Joel David. "Joel" means "Jehovah is God," and "David" means "well beloved." It seemed to fit perfectly.

We dedicated Joel to God that day in a baby dedication service performed at my bedside by the hospital chaplain, with Joel in our arms. We were presented with a small white Bible to us with Joel's footprints on the inside cover along with the Scripture that had been read. They also helped us to make memories with Joel for the few hours we had with him. We took pictures of us holding our little one, and we sang to him. I am so thankful for the memories we were able to make in those few hours. I didn't want to forget anything.

It rained all day, and as we looked out the window of our room, we remember thinking that all of heaven must have been crying with us in our time of great sadness. I have never known such sadness as this; I felt as if my heart had been ripped out and stomped on.

A week later I began to run a fever. At the doctor's office, it was discovered that there was still some tissue in my uterus. I was scheduled for an emergency D & C that same day. After the surgery, I could hear the nurses around me talking. One said, "There was evidence of a second cord." I had been pregnant with twins! I believe that I lost Joel's twin at nine weeks.

Our church helped us move into the new house the week I miscarried, and the church planned a memorial service for the end of the second week to give us an opportunity to say goodbye in our own way. It was really touching to me to see the number of people who came to support us. It was such a blessing to see people we didn't even know very well come to help. We will always be grateful to all those who gave us support; I don't think I can ever say thank you enough.

You may be facing many decisions right now and have no idea what to do. One thing we had to decide was whether to bury Joel or let the hospital dispose of his body. We chose to bury him and had the hospital hold Joel's body until we had a plan. We were able to purchase a plot near my family in southeast Texas, but how to transport him became another problem. The funeral homes wanted $600 to transport him to southeast Texas. We couldn't afford that amount of money, so we decided to pick Joel up the day before the funeral and drive him down. As we left the hospital, I remember thinking, *This is so wrong! I should be carrying my baby out in my arms, not in a book bag!* It was a long drive, and then handing him over to the funeral home when we arrived was almost unbearable. I had bought a little white gown to dress him in and a small teddy bear that would be placed beside him in his casket.

The next day it rained the same as it had the day Joel died. We were convinced once again that heaven was sharing our tears. Our friends from Houston came to be with us. We sang songs that were special to us and that made it so personal. I sang Psalm 121 at the end of the service for him. I needed to sing to him one more time.

The months following Joel's premature delivery were very hard. I could not deal with anything; I could not go anywhere or do anything without crying. Throughout my whole nursing career, I had helped others deal with the crises in their lives, and now I had my own crisis and didn't know what to do.

I didn't understand why God had taken our baby. I felt like He was punishing me and I didn't know why. I then became angry with God and just wanted to walk away from everything I believed. But He was the only safe place to express my true thoughts; after all, He knows them already, right? All I seemed to have were questions, questions and more questions but no answers.

Almost six years later I am sharing this with others. The tears still come—maybe not as often— because we know there is someone missing from our family. But all I know is that God was still there and walked this difficult and sad time with me. I should say He *carried* me, because many times I was not able to stand on my own. Without Him I don't think I would have made it. I believe that as devastating as this was in our lives, God has used it to show me areas in my life and ways of thinking that I need to consider and in some cases change.

I will never know this side of heaven the whys of what happened, but I believe that when Joel opened his eyes for the first time, he saw Jesus! What more could I ask than to know my babies are safe in the arms of Jesus.

Our dear, precious Joel David,

Our hearts ache more than words can say. We had looked forward so much to having you be a part of our lives and then you came so early and left just as fast.

After you were born, we couldn't take our eyes off of you—you were perfect in every way. You were very much like your daddy, in several ways. You were so beautiful, even as tiny as you were; God had perfectly formed you into our son.

They wrapped you in a blanket and let us hold you. Those hours seem so long ago and so short. We now have a lifetime without you, but you will be forever in our hearts.

I don't even begin to understand why God took you from us, but I am thankful for the time He allotted us to spend with you. It was better than nothing. It was so hard to give you back at the end of that day, much less for a lifetime.

Love,
Mommy

Dear Joel,

As I sit down to write this letter to you, I think of your cute little face. I was privileged to be the one to hold you for over an hour after you were born, while your mommy recovered from your birth. As she slept, I gave you a little bath with baby oil. You were such a cute little tyke—all your father's boy. You had my hands, with long slender fingers, my long skinny legs and my big feet. The

memory of these things in you now makes them much more special in me. I now cherish these things, when once I resented them.

Joel, you were such a little blessing even the short time you were with us. Mommy and I really loved you the 15 weeks we had you, even before we met you! We were so looking forward to that! I was especially looking forward to having a boy, so I could be an advocate for you and love you, like a father was meant to love and raise up his son in the Lord. I wanted to hug you and encourage you, be pals with you and hope and pray for you. You will always be our firstborn child and son, and no other child will ever be able to replace you.

Joel, you made such an impact when you arrived, both on us and our wonderful friends and family. Your impact was what God meant for children. You have kept our priorities straight, our eyes moist and our hearts tender and open. These are the blessings of a child.

Although we miss you very much, don't worry, because we are in good hands down here, being very loved and cared for, with many prayers being said for us. While we wish you were here with

us, we have a hope, because we know you
are in a better place, in the loving arms of
Jesus. Joel, we miss you and love you and
look forward to meeting you there someday.

Love,
Your daddy

Way of Pain
BY IKE PATRICK

Lord, You created me wonderfully,
But why must I suffer? Why Christ on a
  tree?
And Lord, You made my inward parts,
But why must we suffer broken hearts?

I know You gave Your Son for me,
But You also took mine, "OH, GOD, LET
  ME BE!!!"
Why do You take babies, too early, too soon—
Why did You rip him from his mother's
  womb?!
A son is all I wanted from You,
But You don't want to give it; it really hurts,
  God, too!

But eleven months later, in an instant, a
  whirl,

You gave us the most precious, beautiful
  girl!
In a little over a month she'll be three
With gorgeous blue eyes and hair that's
  curly.

Now I view life from another perspective:
I can now see why God has to be selective
In the things that He gives us, though we
  plead and we cry,
'Cause it's not always meant for us to know
  why.
But that doesn't mean we'll never have pain;
In fact, we know our hearts will break again.

Jendaya Ryli's Story

Kevin and Erin Rubesh

Jendaya Ryli had red hair and blue eyes. As we held her in our arms, she looked like she was sleeping. A piece of us—that we had been planning for and dreaming about for eight months—had been taken away. In time, we are sure our grief will fade; but for now, it's hard to stop the tears. We're just praying that the Lord will use little Jendaya's death for some good.

Kevin: The morning started out like any other but crashed around our shoulders with an urgent phone call from home. Erin had discovered some blood and was worried. She rushed off to the hospital, where I joined her, but the nurses were unable to find Jendaya's heartbeat.

Erin: Our doctor came in and did an ultrasound, but there were no signs of life. He recommended that I go in for an emergency cesarean section, and I was in the operating room 15 minutes later. One-third of the placenta had separated from the wall of the uterus, and our baby had died.

Kevin: We praise God for a God-fearing doctor. He prayed with us before going into surgery with Erin. As Erin was in the recovery room, I had the chance to sit alone for a while with our baby girl. She was a beautiful little baby—perfect in every way from her red hair to her little toes.

Erin: We're grieving that she never got to meet us—never got to see our faces. But we hope she felt our love for each other and for her as she grew inside me for eight months.

There's one more Rubesh in heaven. We'll miss her for a long time to come, but we trust that someday we'll get to meet her face-to-face in a much better place.

A couple of weeks later, we had a service for our baby girl. We wanted to use the service as an opportunity to let others know of the hope we have in Jesus Christ—the hope of knowing that our little baby Jenna is in the arms of Jesus and that when we die and go to heaven, we'll spend eternity with her! That is a blessing we are looking forward to!

Through it all, we have been working our way through healthy grief. One verse from the Bible was especially meaningful to us:

When you pass through the waters, I will be with you; and when you pass through the rivers, they will not sweep over you. When you walk through the fire, you will not be burned; the flames will not set you ablaze. For I am the LORD, your God, the Holy One of Israel, your Savior (Isa. 43:2-3).

One thing we have learned is not to ask why, since an answer is highly unlikely to come. But instead ask what—what is God teaching us through this? Our marriage has been strengthened through this tragedy, and we definitely are taking fewer things for granted. We are learning to trust Him in *all* things—much easier said than practiced.

We truly have felt the Lord, our God, our Savior, pull us to His chest and hold us tight. The waters were—and still are—deep, but with God's help, they have not swept over us.

Darling Jendaya Ryli,

When you were very small, still inside your mommy, we used to read a story to you. The story was written by Dr. Seuss and it told you about all the exciting things you would see and all the neat people you would meet when you joined us.

Baby, oh baby, the places you'll
    go!
The worlds you will visit! The
    friends you will know![1]

Dear Jenna, we were so looking forward to welcoming you into our family. We had a place all ready for you. Gifts from friends from all over the world. We were going to show you wonderful things and interesting places. We were going to watch you grow, soothe your tears, hold your precious little hands. Your grandma was going to rock you to sleep in her rocking chair. We were going to tell you how much Jesus loved you and how He had made you a special little creation like no other, with beautiful curly red hair and blue eyes. We don't know why, but God had other plans for you *and* for us.

Jenna, when we read to you then and told you how much we loved you, you probably couldn't understand us. But now, Jenna, maybe now you can hear *and* understand the story, so we've changed it a bit—just for you, our precious little girl:

Baby, oh baby,
the place that you'll go!
The heaven you'll visit!
The friends you will know!

Old Moses, just there
with the leathery face
who guided the tribes
through a deserty place.

Noah's the one
with the big wooden boat;
when the floodwaters came,
his zoo went afloat.

You'll sit on the lap
of Esther the queen,
who rescued her people
from someone quite mean.

Daniel will show you
how lions can purr
like big kitty-cats
if you tickle their fur.

You'll play with all of Job's children
and Joseph the dreamer
and Mary and Martha;
You'll catch fish with Peter!

You'll see your aunt Frieda,
not much older than you;
great-grandpas and grandmas
are waiting there, too.

And Jesus will hold you
if you feel alone;
He planned you and made you
Then welcomed you home.

We know that you are in a much better place, Jenna. A place where you'll never feel pain, where you'll never be sad, never have your little heart broken and never lose someone you love. But Jenna—we miss you here. It hurts us so much to see you go before we do—because we love you so much. Your name means thankful, and we are thankful. Thankful that God granted us this all-too-brief encounter with you. Thankful for the excitement and anticipation of your birth. Thankful that your mommy is still alive and healthy. We have so much to be thankful for.

Our dear baby girl, there's a spot in our hearts that will always be saved just for you. And when we finally meet you in heaven, we'll all be together. A happy family. We love you, Jendaya Ryli.

Your mommy and daddy

Joseph's Memorial Service Eulogy

Kyle Duncan

Since May 16, the day that we first learned about Joseph's physical problems, our lives have been changed irrevocably by our son. His presence drilled new shafts into our souls, allowing God to mine more deeply the secret places where earthly light and heavenly peace mix in a sweet, calming balm. Through Joseph, we have more deeply learned the meaning and value of life. Beyond political or cultural rhetoric, we have grasped the reality of the imperishable value of life. What freedom and joy to know, truly know, that every life matters—that our lives matter—that your life matters. Why? Because God designed us and placed us here, now, with these friends, this family, our children, our loved ones.

Our family has learned that the only sure path is the path of complete surrender. When we learned that Joseph would probably not live more than a couple of hours or days, God took us on a severe, merciful journey to a deeper place of submission and obedience. Though we chose the harder road (in the world's eyes) by choosing not to terminate this life, we also learned a priceless secret: True, unadulterated peace and joy is only found when we give way completely and say to God, "I cannot go on without You. I have nothing left of flesh, mind or spirit to offer You. Despite this, Father, I give what I have to You. May You find something of worth in my offering."

If you remember anything of this day, please remember that all things are possible for those who love Christ, for those who are called according to His purpose. Just as Joseph was crippled in body but is now whole in spirit, we also are crippled by the weight of this world, and we can relate to the words of the bard William Shakespeare when troubled Prince Hamlet spoke of his yearning to shuffle off this mortal coil. But though I remain and my son is gone, I know that one thing is true: God has received Joseph into His arms, and one day, we will see him again.

After the death of King David and Bathsheba's newborn son, David says of the boy, "He will not come to me, but I will go to him" (see 2 Sam. 12:23). How liberating to know that God's Word, the Bible, gives evidence to us that we will, as Christians, one day be reunited with our deceased infant children. In gestures of love, many of you have opened up your own hearts and shared about your own lost little ones: babies miscarried, still-born—all taken away too soon. Please take heart, and be comforted to know that God promises in His Word that you will see them again one day.

Suzanne and I and our girls could never, ever repay you, our friends and loved ones, for the precious hours of prayer you invested on our behalf, for Joseph; or for the private, poignant acts of kindness extended our way. While no one else was looking, you extended love, care and compassion—gestures that showed us that yes, the kingdom of God is alive and active and is a present reality.

Today our hearts are mixed with great sadness and great joy, but we know that every life has a story, a testimony, and that Joseph's life has touched thousands, even though it only extended across 3 days, not 30,000 days. I end not with my own words, which falter and could never provide the honorable tribute due my beautiful son, but with the words of Jesus spoken to His disciples:

In my Father's house are many mansions: if it were not so, I would have told you. I go to prepare a place for you. And if I go and prepare a place for you, I will come again, and receive you unto myself; that where I am, there [you] may be also (John 14:2-3, *KJV*).

Good-bye, Joseph. You are loved and will be missed. Yet one day, we will see you again.

Sing to Me
May 21, 2001

I see you, little one.
Feel, touch, taste, smell, hold, grasp.
You touch me
I love you.
You whisper to me in my dreams
And tell me it is alright,
For you have a King
Sitting at your wombside,
Reading to you the story of life.
But not of life on this orbed rock.

The world hears not
Your voice

But it sings—nay, not cries!—to me in the
    darkest hours
When all is quiet and the stars sigh their
    deepest, illumined sighs.
I feel as if I cannot go on, cannot breathe,
    cannot pray, cannot work, cannot sing
Until I touch your face and say good-bye.

But I know that your soul sings to my
    soul;
I feel and taste the song—the taste of
    sweetest manna.
And I know that you whisper, in your
    unsounding voice,
"Daddy, I love you. And I will wait for
    you at the Gate."
My soul cries longingly, deeply, painful-
    ly, for the Gate of Heaven
To open to me, to receive me with you;
But my earthly daughters and wife tug
    at me, wooing me to remain
A man, a father, a provider, a husband,
    a brother, an instrument.
And so I will remain.

Dear Lord,
Do not take away my pain,
For in it, I better understand Yours, as You
    gave up a Son.
Do not take away my grief,

For in it, I more assuredly understand the
    pain of the brokenhearted.
Do not take away my hope,
For without it, I could not go on.

Deepen me—widen this furrow, my God,
That You may plow, seed and farm me.
That I may produce abundance in Your
    name;
That I may die to my own sorrow,
And embrace those who cannot.

Dear Lord,
Seize me.
Hold me.
Sing to me at my soulside,
And read to me the story of life
But not of life on this green, orbed rock.

Teach me the secret chord
That David used to play to please thy
    Lord anew.
And show me how to cut my baby's cord
That he might sing his song for You.

Blessing Elizabeth Bishop's Story

Mark and Jennifer Bishop

We had two healthy little girls already when we discovered God was giving us another child. Both previous pregnancies were healthy, with no complications. This third pregnancy began the same way. In the twenty-sixth week of pregnancy, we went to a routine doctor appointment and sonogram. The sonogram showed disturbing news about the baby: The 26-week-old baby had arms and legs that measured at 21 weeks, lungs at 17 weeks, a 2-vessel umbilical cord instead of a 3-vessel cord and fluid around the lungs and in the brain. The baby's head and body measured appropriately at 26 weeks.

The obstetrician referred us to a perinatologist that very evening for a level 2 sonogram. The perinatologist confirmed the obstetrician's findings and delivered the news that without a miracle from God, the baby would not have a chance to live outside of the uterus due to poor lung development. The perinatologist advised doing an amniocentesis to determine if there was a chromosome abnormality. This determination would tell us whether there was a medical solution to the problems.

We were absolutely in shock with the day's events. All we could do was pray and cry. God, however, was already at work in the situation. We discovered that the perinatologist was a Christian who acknowledged and respected our belief in God and Jesus Christ. She gave us the medical prognosis for our baby, but she also believed God was in control and could perform a miracle if it was in His plan.

The amniocentesis confirmed a humanly uncorrectable chromosome problem with our baby girl. Blood tests also showed that with each pregnancy, we had a 50 percent chance of a problem or miscarriage. We were amazed and grateful for God's granting us two healthy children, but at the same time, we were so sad about the test results.

Even though she was not an advocate for abortion, the perinatologist told us that if we could not handle continuing the pregnancy until birth, she could try to convince the hospital to induce labor early (we were 28 weeks at this point). We knew we could not abort our baby girl. She was alive and kicking, and God had a purpose for her life. Even though we knew God was in control and would grant peace and comfort, we still dealt with the human emotions of despair, sadness and anxiety over having to carry a baby in order to deliver her to die. The perinatalogist confirmed and respected our decision to continue with the pregnancy as long as Jennifer's health was fine.

We began to pray specifically that God would show us what His plan was for our baby. We had to continually give her back to Him. Our little girl was really God's child, whom He was giving us to care for on Earth. We had to let go of trying to control an uncontrollable situation and let God take control.

Within a couple of weeks, God answered our prayers. Jennifer's amniotic fluid level was rising. This meant that the baby was sick and her mother's health was heading for trouble. The doctor told us that if the fluid level continued to rise, Jennifer was at risk for hemorrhaging. It could

be a life-threatening situation if it progressed. We knew our baby would die, but should we risk Jennifer's life, too? We were so saddened with having to begin the grieving process, but we were thankful to God for giving us His direction, so we could begin to prepare. We then began to pray specifically that we would not have to make a decision to terminate our baby's life in order to salvage Jennifer's life. The amniotic fluid level was not dropping, and our little girl was getting worse, not better.

God was and is so gracious and merciful in answering our prayers. At between 30 and 31 weeks, Jennifer went into premature labor. Blessing Elizabeth Bishop was born, lived outside of the uterus for a few minutes and passed back to God in our arms. It was the most humanly painful time of our lives, but we felt God's help and presence so close at hand. God gave us a wonderful hospital nurse and doctor—they shielded us from other labor and delivery patients. What was an awful situation could have been so much worse. We felt God's mercy in our human sorrow.

After returning home from the hospital, we continued our lives amidst raging hormones and grief over a lost child. We realized that when we focused on the human aspect (our loss, missing our baby, not having our child waiting in the crib, not knowing what her favorite color or ice-cream flavor would have been), our grief was huge.

However, when we focused on the God aspect (she is in a better place, healthy, healed, happy, held in the arms of God), we felt peace and comfort. It is amazing how when we focused on ourselves, our grief seemed intensified compared to when we focused on God's grace, love and mercy. However, we did not walk through this time unscathed. We had to go through the grieving, like any other parent who loses a child. We still had those human emotions. We just had to cling to God to take us through the process and beyond the sadness. God allows His time to heal. We had to take that time.

Throughout our trial, we would read the Bible and find some comfort in painful moments. Friends shared passages of encouragement that they'd found, including Psalm 127:3; 139; Isaiah 61; John 14 and James 1:1-18. Reading these passages and having a diligent prayer life and relationship with God provided comfort and healing.

As we reflected on our experience, we realized how God used Blessing's life to further His kingdom. Jennifer's uncle came to know Christ as his personal Savior through our trial. Countless letters and phone calls confirmed how people were touched by God through the experience. We grew closer to our support group of Christian family members and friends. God comforted us through those people who kept contact with us. At a time when a marriage could get rocky, God made ours stronger by forcing us to lean on each other through Him and let go of our individual control. Even though Blessing was on Earth for a fraction of time, God had a purpose for her life! We were fortunate to witness the fruit of her life from God.

Looking back and remembering how God answered our prayers, cared for us and worked to glorify Himself took away the terrible sting and bitterness of hurt over time. We will always miss our little girl. There will always be the proverbial place at the dinner table for her. However, we know that she is in heaven. We will see her again. God's plan was just different from our plan, and God was and is still glorified by His plan for Blessing's life.

It has been over a year since Blessing went to heaven, and we still think of her often. However, we reflect on her with sweetness rather than pain. God has enabled us to empathize, understand and comfort others who are experiencing the loss of a child. We would not have had that insight had we not had the experience of Blessing.

God's love has also overwhelmed us, leading us to become foster parents. Since we wanted an addition to our family, Jennifer's mother suggested we look into foster parenting. (The need is huge!) We probably would not have considered the program without going through a loss experience. Now we feel called to foster other children in need. We can relate to their loss of parents. Someday, we may even adopt one of the children. Who knows what

God has planned! All we know is that as long as we keep our eyes on Him, He will continue to work in our lives and further His kingdom.

Dearest Blessing,

Hi, sweet girl! We love you and miss you. Your sisters, Hannah and Tabitha, love you and miss you, too! In fact, you look a lot like Hannah. Isn't that neat! They enjoy talking about how you are in heaven with God and Jesus. We are so glad you are healed and happy. God will hold on to you for us. Someday, we will join you, and what a fun time it will be!

Through your life, God has changed our lives. It is amazing how God truly has a purpose for every life He creates. Through knowing you, we came to know God better. Our entire family grew closer to God and to each other. Now we are serving others for God in ways we never would have imagined. We are so thankful to God for your life and what your life experience has taught us. God loves you more than we could ever love you, and that is a lot!

We can't wait to hold you again, sweetie!

Love,
Mommy and Daddy

A LETTER TO NEIMAN FROM MOM

Ramona McKissic

Dearest Neiman,

I am your mom. I am writing you this letter to let you know how much you blessed our lives with your presence. I have told our story a million times to just about any soul who will listen.

Your daddy and I had been trying to conceive you for about 18 months, and I was getting very depressed. We often thought it was not God's will for us to have another child. I remember going to the altar for special prayer at a women's conference. I received prayer and stood on my belief that God would allow me to conceive you. Needless to say, about six weeks later I was at the zoo with your big brother, Nykolas Ryen, and walked through a cave with aquariums. I came out the other side very nauseated. I returned home and took a home pregnancy test and confirmed my suspicions. We were *very* happy. I immediately made an appointment with the same doctor who had delivered your brother.

I went to the doctor about three weeks later. He confirmed the pregnancy and gave a due date of December 25, 2000. Imagine, on Christmas Day I would have a gift better than anything I could have ever dreamed! I immediately told everyone in the family and at the office. I purchased diapers after I came back from that first doctor visit. I felt in my heart of hearts that you were another very special baby boy like your brother. You were named after I returned home from the zoo trip. I went on with my daily routine of working, cooking, cleaning and keeping up with Nykolas. A month or so later, I went to Austin for a managers' training class for three weeks. The entire class ate crackers and drank soda with you and me in the morning hours. I was happy. My clothes were starting to feel snug in the waist.

I returned from the training class and was home for two days when I got sick. I did the laundry that evening after work. I ate some milk and cookies and went to bed. I thought that I was having gas pains, but the end result was that you were not well. I was in utter shock and in a state of disbelief. I did not want to believe that the soul inside me, that had so much blessed me, was trying to leave me. I was not bleeding on the outside, but I felt that something was wrong on the inside because of the horrible pain. I endured the pain through the night. By morning, I had come to the realization that something was wrong with you. With my heart hurting and my eyesight gone (I could only see yellow), passing in and out of consciousness due to blood loss, I prayed to God to come see about us and let His will be done in our lives.

Your daddy called 9-1-1, and your granny (my mother) beat the ambulance to the house. I only remember bits and pieces about the next week. I remember the doctor telling my husband and mother that she would try to save me, but she didn't know if she could. I don't think I regained consciousness that day, but late the next day I woke up. I had relatives from far away with me. Your other granny from Illinois even came to see about you and me.

I know that a lot of what I am saying to you sounds so sad and tragic. Son, I promise you the only thing that is remotely close to tragic is that I cannot hug you right now at this moment. I know that everything in our lives happens according to God's time, not our time. He has promised me that I will be allowed all the hugs and kisses in heaven that I am not able to experience with you here on Earth.

You healed so many wounded areas in my life. Your daddy and my daddy (your papaw) had a very strained relationship due to an argument that happened in 1991. They were only cordial to one another because they had no choice. When this happened, I remember waking up to see your daddy and Papaw standing side by side by my bed, crying. Their relationship is so much better now. You also brought your daddy and his mother closer. You helped Daddy realize how important family is and not to take it for granted.

I did not totally understand why you had to leave me when you did or why I did not go with you. I did not understand your expected birth date of Christmas Day. Now I understand it all much more clearly. You came to heal the wounded areas in my life. You took away my spirit of discouragement and replaced it with *joy*. You helped me understand and appreciate my life. I understand the significance of Christmas Day. God fixed it so that for the rest of my life I would not have to mark the calendar to remember. There is not a day that passes that I don't think of you in some small way.

I also now understand that I could not go with you because I had to stay and be here for

your daddy and brother. Your granny on daddy's side died just seven months after you left us. She was 51 years old. You had to go on so that she would not be scared or afraid when she got there. If I had gone with you, Daddy would have probably moved to Illinois so that she could help him with Nykolas, and then she would have died just seven months later. You know that she did not have any daughters. I had to plan her funeral and clean out her things. I hope you get to know your granny. She was a great mother-in-law and an even better granny. Give her a kiss for us.

I miss you dearly. I know that I will see you again. I dream of you sometimes and feel that you come to me to let me know you are happy. I love you with all of my heart. Thank you.

Mom

Rebekah's Story of Jonathan

June 24, 1995, is a day that will forever be etched in my mind. I will always remember the hushed yet panicked and grief-stricken conversations of that hot Texas afternoon.

Six years earlier, I was diagnosed with a congenital kidney disease and was told I would eventually need a kidney transplant. My husband, Byron, and I had been married seven months, and children were definitely part of our future plans. Two years after diagnosing me, my kidney specialist gave his approval for us to begin a family. Despite a few complications and 10 weeks of bed rest, on November 1, 1991, I gave birth to a healthy baby boy whom we named Byron, Jr.

Shortly after Byron, Jr.'s third birthday, we conceived our second child. Unlike my experience of carrying Byron, Jr., with this baby, the complications began very early in the pregnancy. My obstetrican told me, "If you are having this kind of trouble so early, we have a long road ahead of us. And, Rebekah, I have to tell you, if things don't get better, we will have to end the pregnancy."

Miraculously, over the next several weeks my blood pressure stabilized and I began preparing for the late summer due date. In the middle of my second trimester, an ultrasound revealed that my baby was a boy. Byron and I named our unborn son Jonathan, meaning "precious gift from God."

Close to my third and final trimester, blood work revealed that the pregnancy was putting a strain on my already-weak kidneys, and they were undoubtedly losing function. At 23 weeks gestation, my obstetrician ordered me to bed rest. Twenty-seven weeks into the pregnancy, the doctor phoned to tell me he felt I needed to be hospitalized and the baby should be delivered.

Byron, my parents and I arrived at Methodist Medical Center in Dallas early the next morning. I checked in at labor and delivery, where we consulted with my obstetrician, my nephrologist, a neonatologist and a perinatologist. We were informed that the baby was in no danger and, in fact, was very healthy and strong; yet if he were to be delivered that day, he had an approximate 80 percent chance of survival and would likely suffer many side effects. Thankfully, the team of doctors agreed that it wasn't necessary to promptly deliver Jonathan, but I should be admitted and carefully monitored. Later that afternoon I was taken to the same room where I had spent two weeks of my pregnancy with Byron, Jr.

I was very thankful for every extra day that helped Jonathan's little body grow and mature. Occasionally my little son, Byron Jr., was allowed to spend the night at the hospital. On Friday, June 23, little Byron snuggled next to me all night, with Jonathan, still safe in my womb, between us.

The next morning, my husband had a meeting and left the hospital early. I took my morning pills, assuming that I would eat shortly, and climbed back into bed. Within a few minutes I became severely nauseated and began throwing up. Because Little Byron was still with me, I didn't call the nurse for fear she would never again allow him to stay. Instead, I paged Byron and told him to immediately get back to the hospital.

Feeling somewhat better, I crawled back into bed with my sleeping little boy. As I turned to cud-

dle with him, Jonathan began violently kicking inside of me. I rubbed my tummy and said aloud, "What's the matter, Jon-Jon?" Lying on my left side, I then felt what I assumed was Jonathan's body float up toward my right side.

Just after noon my nephrologist came in to tell me he could not let the pregnancy continue. My lab report was not good, and if my kidneys were allowed to endure the stress of maintaining the pregnancy much longer, they would fail. He was still in my room talking to Byron and me when my nurse came in to take routine vitals, which included listening to the baby's heartbeat. After a couple of minutes, she looked up at the doctor and nonchalantly said she could not hear any heart tones. Assuming that we were making too much noise, he laughingly said he was leaving. The nurse left to find another Doppler. When she returned, she brought another nurse with her.

Unaware of the seriousness of the situation, we continued talking and laughing and thought it was cute that Jonathan was "hiding" from the nurses. They both tried for a few more minutes to hear something and then abruptly left the room. Within seconds the same nurses whisked back into the room, turned off the lights and shut the curtains. Before I knew it, my room was filled with medical staff. I was instantly hooked up to a fetal monitor and tried to sort through the myriad orders. I heard something about an "IV . . . the operating room . . . call her family . . . STAT" and so on. Suddenly my obstetrician walked through the door.

Someone crashed a gurney through the door, and another person come toward me with an armload of needles, IV lines and saline bags. Fearing that this would cause my blood pressure to soar, my obstetrician told everyone to calm down, take the gurney out and not start an IV. I managed to find Byron's face in the crowd, and after seeing his crestfallen expression, I turned my head to view the sonogram screen. I saw the form of my baby. He was still and limp, his arm dangling to his side. I knew my baby was dead.

Slowly and quietly, those who remained in my room turned off the machines, bowed their heads and left. My obstetrician and one nurse stayed behind. He explained that he would need to deliver the baby. Thankfully I could deliver by cesarean section that night.

As soon as the door shut behind my doctor, I burst into tears and repeatedly told Byron that I was sorry. I felt I had failed my baby, my husband, my family and everyone I knew.

One by one my family members arrived at the hospital. A nurse explained to us that we could—and should—hold our baby, encouraged us to take pictures and even offered to let him stay in the room with us for as long as we wished. At the

time, I could not imagine bringing my dead baby back to my room.

Several hours later, I was in the operating room with Byron next to me, just as he had been when Byron, Jr., was born. Unlike giving birth to a live baby who cries, there is no way of knowing when a stillborn baby is delivered. The silence is deafening! Upon delivery my obstetrician had to untangle the umbilical cord that was snaked around Jonathan's head, body and left leg—the culprit of his demise. His lifeline of 29 weeks in my womb was the assailant.

I will never forget when the nurse walked in with my lifeless, otherwise-perfect, 2-pound, 12-ounce baby swaddled in her arms and handed him to me. It was so natural to reach out and take him from her as if she were bringing him to me for a feeding. He was absolutely beautiful, with perfect little features that were identical to his big brother's. I held Jonathan close to my face, kissed his head, examined every part of his little body and told him I loved him.

Once we had spent some time with the baby alone, we wanted to share him with our family, who were waiting in an empty birthing room down the hall. I am forever grateful for the time our parents, sisters, brothers and pastors were privileged to spend with my son. Several of them had cameras and, thankfully, took the liberty of snapping pictures of different family members holding the baby. Our pastor, J. Don George, led us in a sweet time of prayer as he held our infant in his arms. He thanked the Lord for Jonathan and for the peace and assurance we had in knowing he was in heaven.

Five days after giving birth, we buried our baby. Sitting underneath that white tent and staring at my baby's tiny satin coffin was surreal. I could not believe the child I had prayed for—my miracle baby—was gone. Surely this was a bad dream from which I would soon awaken!

It didn't take long for the shock to wear off and the grief to penetrate like a bullet. Every part of my body ached for my baby. At times I thought I was going crazy with the phantom kicks I continued to feel, the cries I heard in the middle of the night and the continuous dreams that the hospital had made a terrible mistake and Jonathan was alive after all.

I silently became angry with everyone—myself, my family, my friends, strangers and, most of all, God. I felt so cheated and betrayed by Him. How could He have allowed something like this to happen? Did I not have enough faith? Did I do something wrong? Was I not a good enough mom? I desperately longed to talk with another mother who had endured a similar loss.

The loss of Jonathan caused me to question everything I had ever believed about my faith and God's goodness. From my perspective, my closest friend had become not only a stranger, but honestly I perceived Him also as an enemy. I found myself unable to pray and unwilling to let Him be my comfort and strength. All the while though, I continued to put on my mask at church—I hosted monthly care groups in our home and I went through the motions of acting like a Christian. However, there were days when I questioned God's very existence.

These immense feelings of loneliness and spiritual struggle lasted almost a year. Finally, on Mother's Day, of all days, I opened my heart to the Lord and He filled me with peace, comfort and joy. Truly God turned my mourning into dancing and filled my mouth with a new song of praise! Did I ever have a bad day again? Absolutely! But the anger dissipated and the thoughts and memories became bittersweet instead of incredibly painful, and I knew the Lord had a plan.

His purpose began to unfold over the next few weeks. One Sunday afternoon, just before Jonathan's one-year anniversary in heaven, I felt compelled to browse the obituary section of the newspaper. Never having done that before, I felt somewhat morbid looking for an announcement of a baby's death. To my surprise, I found one. I instantly knew that I was supposed to contact the grieving mother to let her know that I, too, had experienced a stillbirth and was available to talk with her if she so desired. Two days after mailing her a card, she e-mailed me and expressed her gratitude that a complete stranger would reach out to her. We eventually met for lunch, and for hours we shared our feelings, thoughts and emotions.

Because I found her through the newspaper obituaries, it inspired her to attempt to do the same for someone else. She met another grieving mom, then another and yet another. Before long we had all become friends and began meeting with each other on a regular basis. After several weeks of this, it occurred to me that we had begun an infant loss support group; and I named it M.E.N.D., which stands for Mommies Enduring Neonatal Death. With the help of my attorney father, we soon obtained our nonprofit status and became a legitimate organization. We adapted 2 Corinthians 1:4 as the theme for M.E.N.D., which says that we can comfort those in any trouble with the comfort we ourselves have received from God.

Soon we began publishing newsletters, which currently are distributed all over the world. We started hosting an official share group and now offer five different varieties of support every month. A website was created for M.E.N.D., which has enabled grieving parents from all parts of the globe to seek Christian support. Twice a year we gather for commemorative ceremonies to remember our babies. On many occasions I have been honored to speak at hospital conferences and workshops as well as mother's groups, educating them on how to respond when parents lose a baby.

I admit that at times it's hard not to question, and sometimes I still ask why. But I've learned that God is God and His ways are higher than ours (see Isa. 55:9). I believe that when we get to heaven, it will all be revealed. First Corinthians 13:12 promises, "Now we see but a poor reflection as in a mirror; then we shall see face to face." We could all waste away trying to make sense of life's sufferings, but I believe that God gently warned us against this in Deuteronomy 29:29 when He said that the secret things belong to Him.

Baby Huxham

Sharon Huxham

My life is but a weaving between my Lord and me;
I cannot choose the colors, He worketh steadily.
Oft times He weaveth sorrow and I in foolish pride
Forget He sees the upper and I the underside.
The dark threads are as needful in the
weaver's skillful hand,
As the threads of gold and silver in the
pattern He has planned.
Not till the loom is silent and the shuttle ceases to fly,
Shall God unroll the canvas and explain
the reason why.

AUTHOR UNKNOWN

We were enjoying life as a family of three—with a one-year old—when we were surprised by a sec-ond pregnancy. Initially I thought it was not the right time, but I realized that God would work out the details of having two children so close in age. We were adjusting to thoughts of a family of three becoming four when I began spotting. Four days later I miscarried. Our baby was gone. That was 11 years ago.

God is good. I knew that. God is in control. I knew that. God always has a plan that we often cannot see. I knew that. When I awoke from the D & C, I knew those things definitively; however, I was filled with a wrenching pain never before experienced. Grief overwhelmed me. I had lost a child, dreams and some of my future. The first days were agonizing as I searched for comfort in the Scriptures.

I love the LORD, for he heard my voice; he heard my cry for mercy. The cords of death entangled me, the anguish of the grave came upon me; I was overcome by trouble and sorrow. Then I called on the name of the LORD: "O LORD, save me!" The Lord is gracious and righteous; our God is full of compassion. . . . When I was in great need, he saved me" (Ps. 116:1,3-6).

I was not disappointed. God met my need by cry-ing with me. He wrapped His arms around my hurting heart and said, "I care."

Through the next weeks and months, I found that losing a child so early was a lonely kind of grief. Family and friends haven't felt the bond a mother feels, and therefore the loss is felt less deeply. It was hard. A secret pal wrote me a note during those weeks. She had lost three children to miscarriage and wrote: "The Lord will carry you over your hurt, then through it, and finally past it—but you'll never forget."

The Lord was faithful to meet my hurting heart in deep grief. He slowly mended that heart over the months that came. We moved across the country a few months later. I met a new friend named Debbie, who was such an encouragement during those days of transition. I had no idea God was preparing to teach us both. Debbie lost a baby within months of our meeting. God allowed me to be a source of encouragement to her as she walked through her valley of grief. As I encouraged her, He continued to heal my hurting heart.

I thank God for allowing this loss to be used for His glory by helping me comfort other mothers who are walking through the "valley of the shadow of death" (Ps. 23:4). After all these years, the memories can unexpectedly flood me with grief. However, He has been faithful to bring me past that grief to a new understanding of His everlasting arms of love.

DEAR LITTLE ONE,

I walked a mile with Pleasure,
She chattered all the way.
But she left me none the wiser
For all she had to say.
I walked a mile with Sorrow
And ne'er a word said she.
But, oh, the things I learned from her
When Sorrow walked with me.[2]

I praise God for what He used you to do in my life. He is sufficient for anything that comes my way. He loves me deeply. He is always faithful, and He works all for my good and His glory.

Your loving mommy

YOUR STORY

Your journey began with the excitement and expectation of bringing a new life into this world. Then, suddenly, the journey detoured through loss. It is my prayer that your journey today is taking you on to new roads called healing and hope. It is time for you to write about your unique experiences. I invite you to use the next few pages to express what is in your heart. If you like, review your journal entries at the end of each chapter to remind you of where you have walked and what you have felt along the way. You can express your story in a variety of ways. Perhaps you will write a eulogy or a song or a poem that communicates your deepest feelings about the loss of your baby. You can even write a love letter that says everything you wish you could say to your little one who awaits you in heaven. —DH

_____

_____

_____

_____

_____

_____

_____

_____

_____

ENDNOTES

Chapter 2
1. Pam Vredevelt, *Empty Arms* (Sisters, OR: Multnomah Publishers, 1994), pp. 9-10.

Chapter 3
1. Mary Jane Worden, *Women's Devotional Bible* (Grand Rapids, MI: Zondervan Publishing House, 1990), p. 218. See also Mary Jane Worden, *Early Widow* (Nashville, TN: Word Publishing, 1989).
2. See website descriptions, book recommendations and music lists in Resources section in the back of this book.

Chapter 5
1. George Matheson, "The Thorns" from *Streams in the Desert* (Grand Rapids, MI: Zondervan Publishing House, 1997), n.p.

Chapter 6
1. Chuck Swindoll, *Hope Again: When Life Hurts and Dreams Fade* (Nashville, TN: Word Publishing, 1997), n.p.
2. C. S. Lewis, *The Last Battle* (New York: HarperCollins Publishers, 1994), n.p.
3. Dr. John MacArthur, Jr., *The Salvation of Babies Who Die*, Bible Bulletin Board GC 80-242, audiocassette.

Stories of Loss, Healing and Hope
1. Tish Rabe and Theodor Seuss Geisel, *Oh, the Places You'll Go!* (New York: Random House, 1990), n.p.
2. Robert Browning Hamilton, "Along the Road."

Resources

GRIEF MATERIALS

Birth and Life Bookstore
141 Commercial Street NE
Salem, Oregon 97301
(503) 371-4445
(800) 443-9942
http://bookstore.1cascade.com

Provides a vast selection of books and videos covering all aspects of birth, alternative health and parenting. Call for a catalog or order from their website.

Centering Corporation
P.O. Box 4600
Omaha, NE 68104
(402) 553-1200
Fax: (402) 553-0507
www.centering.org

Provides literature on death, dying and coping with bereavement issues, including infant loss and death of children. Catalog available on request.

ICEA Bookmarks
P.O. Box 20048
Minneapolis, MN 55420
(800) 624-4934
www.icea.org/bkmks.htm

ICEA Bookmarks publishes a catalog twice yearly, listing books, posters, audiocassettes, videocassettes, pamphlets and booklets by topic on the subjects of childbirth, family-centered maternity care, breast-feeding and early child care.

Perinatal Loss Project
2116 NE 18th Avenue
Portland, OR 97212
(503) 284-7426
www.griefwatch.com

Booklets, cards and videos available for purchase.

Wintergreen Press

3630 Eileen Street

Maple Plain, MN 55359

(952) 476-1303

www.wintergreenpress.com

Provides books, booklets, audiovisual materials and consultant/trainer on the subject of miscarriage and infant loss.

If you would like to stop mailings or calls from baby suppliers to your home, you can remove your name from promotional lists by contacting the following. (This will not stop every mailing or call, but it will catch the bulk. It may take several weeks to take effect.)

Mailing Lists:

Direct Marketing Association

Mail Reference Service

P.O. Box 9008

Farmingdale, NY 11735

Telephone Solicitations:

Direct Marketing Association

Phone Reference Service

P.O. Box 9014

Farmingdale, NY 11735

Internet Sites

www.angelsinheaven.org—**Angels in Heaven Ministries** is a nonprofit, nondenominational, Christ-centered ministry dedicated to sharing the hope of Jesus Christ with families who have suffered the loss of a loved one, particularly that of a child. Our ministry is accomplished through unique memory keepsakes and cards, personal Scripture-based counseling and informing and equipping others to minister effectively at times of loss.

www.babyloss.com—**Babyloss** is an online resource providing advice and support in the areas of pregnancy loss, stillbirth or neonatal death. Tries to point visitors to particular organizations or individuals that will be of specific help.

www.climb-support.org—**Center for Loss in Multiple Birth, Inc.** is by and for parents who have experienced the death of one or more or all of their twins, triplets or higher multiples at any time from conception through childhood. It is a national and international group and offers a quarterly newsletter (print) and parent contact list (not online).

www.galaxymall.com/children/angelbabies—**Angel Babies in Heaven Memorials** provides infant memorials, memorial stones and assorted keepsakes, and pregnancy loss, stillbirth, miscarriage and infant death support.

www.geocities.com/threadsofhope—This website provides information about the Bible study, *Threads of Hope, Pieces of Joy,* which has been written especially for those who have experienced unintentional pregnancy loss. In addition, this site has personal stories and information about the authors, Teale Fackler and Gwen Kik.

www.godslittleones.com—**God's Little Ones** is a Christian, pro-life art gallery of original, and medically accurate, hand-cast, hand-painted resin portrait dolls made in the likeness of real babies born at 7 to 36 weeks gestation and beyond. *Hold the beauty of life in the palm of your hand!*

www.groups.yahoo.com/group/ourlossheavensgain—This is a Christian online message support group for mothers who have lost their child(ren) to miscarriage, ectopic pregnancy, stillbirth or neonatal death.

www.hannah.org—**Hannah's Prayer Ministries** provides Christian support for those who have experienced infertility or infant death at any time from conception through early infancy.

www.handonline.org—**Helping After Neonatal Death** is a nonprofit corporation founded in 1981 to help parents, their families and their healthcare providers cope with the loss of a baby before, during or after birth. There are no fees for their services.

www.mend.org—**M.E.N.D.** (Mommies Enduring Neonatal Death) is a Christian nonprofit organization that reaches out to families who have lost a baby through miscarriage, stillbirth or early infant death.

www.missfoundation.org—**The M.I.S.S. Foundation** is a nonprofit international organization providing immediate and ongoing support to grieving families. It encourages proactive community involvement and volunteerism and the reduction of infant and toddler death through research and education.

www.nationalshareoffice.com—**SHARE** is a not-for-profit nondenominational organization providing support for those who have experienced the death of a baby through early pregnancy loss, stillbirth or newborn death.

www.pregnancyandinfantloss.com—**Remembering Our Babies** is the official site of Pregnancy and Infant Loss Remembrance Day, October 15th of every year. If you have suffered a miscarriage, ectopic pregnancy, stillbirth or the loss of an infant, you and all of the other parents, grandparents, siblings, relatives and friends have a special day of remembrance.

www.quietrefuge.com—**A Quiet Refuge** seeks to address the needs of families who have experienced the loss of an infant or preborn child. This web site offers a small photojournal album in which families can place pictures and memorabilia, as well as journal thoughts, to remember and honor the brief but precious lives of their little ones.

www.rivendell.org—**GriefNet** offers help and support through e-mail support groups. Resources including books, leaflets, videocassettes and audiocassettes are also available, as well as a library containing articles on various aspects of grief and bereavement (how to cope with grief during holidays, how children grieve, gender differences and grief, etc.). GriefNet also provides information on locating hospices, support groups, funeral homes, counselors and retreats; contact information for your region; related Internet sites; and memorials.

www.sandswa.org.au—**SIDS and Kids** provides support, information and encouragement to anyone who has been affected by the sudden and unexpected death of a child from conception to 2 years of age, from any cause.

www.sids-network.org—This site, the growing collaborative effort of individuals from across the United States and around the world, offers up-to-date information as well as support for those who have been touched by the tragedy of **Sudden Infant Death Syndrome and Other Infant Death** (SIDS/OID).

www.txmomsoftinyangels.org—**Texas Moms of Tiny Angels** is a nonprofit pregnancy and infant loss awareness and support organization. It supports families that have suffered the loss of miscarriage, stillbirth and/or early infant death. The site includes grief resource materials, songs, poetry, a memorial garden, ways to create memories of your babies and a way to meet other bereaved parents.

BOOKS

Allen, Marie, and Shelly Marks. *Miscarriage: Women Sharing from the Heart.* Somerset, NJ: John Wiley and Sons, 1993.

Bauman, Harold. *How Do I Live Through Grief.* Uhrichsville, OH: Barbour Publishing, 2000.

Cohn, Janice, and Gail Owens. *Molly's Rosebush.* Morton Grove, IL: Albert Whitman & Co., 1994.

Davis, Deborah L. *Empty Cradle, Broken Heart: Surviving the Death of Your Baby*. Golden, CO: Fulcrum Publishing, 1996.

DeYmaz, Linda. *Mommy, Please Don't Cry*. Sisters, OR: Multnomah Publishing, 1997.

Dobson, James. *When God Doesn't Make Sense*. Wheaton, IL: Tyndale House Publishers, 2001.

Fackler, Teale, and Gwen Kik. *Threads of Hope, Pieces of Joy: A Pregnancy Loss Bible Study*. Benjamin Books, 1999.

Guthrie, Nancy. *Holding On to Hope*. Wheaton, IL: Tyndale House Publishers, 2002.

Hayford, Jack. *I'll Hold You in Heaven*. Ventura, CA: Regal Books, 2003.

Hey, Valerie, ed. *Hidden Loss: Miscarriage and Ectopic Pregnancy*. London, England: Womens Press, Ltd., 1997.

Hinton, Clara. *Silent Grief*. Green Forest, AR: New Leaf Press, 1998.

Ilse, Sherokee, ed. *Empty Arms*. Maple Plain, MN: Wintergreen Press, 2000.

——, and Linda Hammer Burns. *Miscarriage: A Shattered Dream*. Maple Plain, MN: Wintergreen Press, 1992.

Ingram, Christine J. *Always Precious in Our Memory; Reflections After Miscarriage, Stillbirth or Neonatal Death*. Chicago: ACTA Publications, 1999.

Keaggy, Bernadette. *Losing You Too Soon*. Eugene, OR: Harvest House Publishers, 2002.

Kraybill, Nelson, and Ellen Kraybill. *Miscarriage: A Quiet Grief*. Scottdale, PA: Herald Press, 1990.

Lafser, Christine O'Keeffe, and Phyllis Tickle. *An Empty Cradle, a Full Heart*. Chicago: Loyola Press, 1998.

Luebbermann, Mimi. *Coping with Miscarriage: A Simple, Reassuring Guide to Emotional and Physical Healing*. Roseville, CA: Prima Publishing, 1994.

Morrow, Judy, and Nancy Gordon. *Silent Cradle*. Indianapolis, IN: Light and Life Communications, 1998.

Page, Carole Gift. *Misty: Our Momentary Child*. Wheaton, IL: Crossway Books, 1987.

Peppers, Larry G., and Ronald J. Knapp. *How to Go On Living After the Death of a Baby*. Atlanta, GA: Peachtree Publishers, 1985.

Rank, Maureen. *Free to Grieve*. Minneapolis, MN: Bethany House, 1985.

Reid, Joanie. *Life Line: A Journal for Parents Grieving a Miscarriage, Stillbirth or Other Early Infant Death*. Sarasota, FL: Pineapple Press, 1994.

Schweibert, Pat, M.D., and Paul Kirk. *When Hello Means Goodbye*. Portland, OR: Perinatal Loss Grief Watch, 1993.

Smith, Harold Ivan. *Decembered Grief*. Kansas City, MO: Beacon Hill Press, 1999.

Stetson, Brad. *Tender Fingerprints*. Grand Rapids, MI: Zondervan Publishing House, 1999.

Swindoll, Charles. *Hope Again*. Nashville, TN: Word Publishing, 1997.

Tengbom, Mildred. *Grief for a Season*. Minneapolis,

MN: Bethany House, 1989.

Vredevelt, Pam. *Empty Arms: Emotional Support for Those Who Have Suffered Miscarriage or Stillbirth*. Sisters, OR: Multnomah Press, 2001.

Westberg, Granger. *Good Grief*. Minneapolis, MN: Augsburg Fortress Press, 1986.

Wheat, Rick. *Miscarriage: A Man's Book*. Omaha, NE: Centering Corp., 1995.

Winnenburg, Kathe. *Grieving the Child I Never Knew*. Grand Rapids, MI: Zondervan Publishing House, 2001.

Yancey, Philip. *Disappointment with God*. Grand Rapids, MI: Zondervan Publishing House, 1997.

Music

Name of song: "A Visitor from Heaven"
Title of CD: *Beyond A Dream*
Performer: Twila Paris
Lyrics and Music: Twila Paris

Name of song: "Angel Unaware"
Title of audiocassette: "Angel Unaware" (single recording)
Performer: Brook Buie
Lyrics and Music: Shari Buie and Tamara Miller
To order: www.angelsinheaven.org

Name of song: "Blessing in the Thorn"
Title of CD: *Where Strength Begins*
Performer: Phillips, Craig & Dean
Lyrics and Music: Randy Phillip, Dave Clark and Dan Koch

Name of song: "Empty Arms"
Title of CD: *Look Ahead*
Performer: Teri Curp
Lyrics and Music: Teri Curp

Name of song: "Glory Baby"
Title of CD: *All Things New*
Performer: Watermark
Lyrics and Music: Nathan and Christy Nockels

Name of song: "Goodbye for Now"
Title of CD: *Corner of Eden*
Performer: Kathy Troccoli
Lyrics and Music: Kathy Troccoli

Name of song: "His Strength Is Perfect"
Title of CD: *Real Life Conversations*
Performer: Steven Curtis Chapman
Lyrics and Music: Steven Curtis Chapman and Jerry Salley

Name of song: "Home Free"
Title of CD: *Home Free*
Performer: Home Free
Lyrics and Music: Wayne Watson

Name of song: "Jesus Will Still Be There"
Title of CD: *Point of Grace*
Performer: Point of Grace
Lyrics and Music: Robert Sterling and John Mandeville

Name of song: "My Life Is in Your Hands"
Title of CD: *Kathy Troccoli*
Performer: Kathy Troccoli
Lyrics and Music: Kathy Troccoli and Bill Montvilo

Name of song: "Ryan's Song"
Title of CDs: *Time 2, Way Back Home* and *Phil Keaggy reEmerging*
Performer: Phil Keaggy
Lyrics and Music: Phil Keaggy and Bill Clarke

Name of song: "We Thought You'd Be Here"
Title of CD: *A Room Full of Stories*
Performer: Wes King
Lyrics and Music: Wes King

Name of song: "With Hope"
Title of CDs: *Speechless* and *Diving In*
Performer: Steven Curtis Chapman
Lyrics and Music: Steven Curtis Chapman

Name of song: "Why?"
Title of CDs: *Best Ones* and *Face the Nation*
Performer: 4Him
Lyrics and Music: Dave Clark, Don Koch and Randy Phillips

Angels in Heaven Ministries

Bringing Comfort & Peace in Times of Grief

Christian Bookstores

Hospitals

Pastors

Women's Ministries

Bereavement Support
Groups and Services

Pregnancy Resource
Centers

Stephen Ministries

Christian Counselors

Friends

Families

Memory Keepsakes

Angels in Heaven Ministries is a Christ-centered, non-profit ministry dedicated to sharing the hope of Christ with those who have experienced the loss of a loved one.

Our line of unique Memory Keepsakes can be given as treasured gifts that provide opportunities to reach out to one another in times of grief.

A keepsake not only serves as a physical reminder of a precious life, but also provides families with a way to honor a life worth remembering!

Available at Christian bookstores or online at www.angelsinheaven.org

Angels in Heaven Ministries • P.O. Box 868115 • Plano, TX 75086-8115
972-424-5508 • Fax: 972-881-9950 • info@angelsinheaven.org • www.angelsinheaven.org

Angels in Heaven Ministries

Author & Speaker

Debbie Heydrick is passionate about sharing the comfort and peace of Jesus Christ with those who have experienced a loss.

Debbie captivates audiences with her gentle smile, compassionate heart and angelic voice. With an eternal perspective, she shares her personal testimony of loss, healing and hope through singing and speaking to audiences of all sizes.

Her Message:
- · empathizes with personal loss
- · validates & gives permission to grieve
- · encourages through scripture
- · acknowledges the sanctity of the unborn
- · equips others to reach out in times of loss

To invite Debbie to speak at your church, special event or conference, call 972-424-5508 or email debbie@angelsinheaven.org

Bringing Comfort & Peace in Times of Grief

Memory Book

A Special Baby's Memory Book by Dorothy Ferguson. For parents of stillborn infants or those who die shortly after birth. Features a journal for feelings, memorable dates, pictures, place for mementos, last moments, and your story: the day you were born. 24 pages that includes gentle poems.

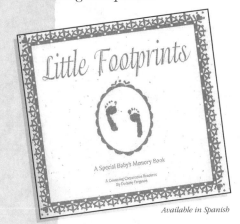

Available in Spanish

Call for a catalog of grief resources.

Centering Corporation
PO Box 4600
Omaha, NE 68104

Phone: 402-553-1200
Fax: 402-553-0507

E-mail: centeringcorp@aol.com
Online resources: www.centering.org

The Classic Best-Seller—Over 250,000 In Print

I'LL HOLD YOU IN HEAVEN

*Healing and Hope for the Parent Who has
Lost a Child through Miscarriage, Stillbirth,
Abortion or Early Infant Death*

JACK HAYFORD

I'll Hold You in Heaven
Healing and Hope for the Parent Who Has Lost a Child
Through Miscarriage, Stillbirth, Abortion or Early Infant Death
Jack Hayford
Mass • ISBN 08307.32594

Regal
God's Word for Your World™